Understanding
Chernobyl

Understanding Chernobyl

THE URANIUM INSTITUTE
LONDON

Published by The Uranium Institute, Twelfth Floor, Bowater House, 68 Knightsbridge, London SW1X 7LT

ISBN 0 946777 09 8

Produced by A. E. Thompson Publishing Services, London
Set by Pentacor Ltd., High Wycombe, Bucks
Printed and bound in Great Britain by
Redwood Burn Limited, Trowbridge, Wiltshire

Foreword

This booklet brings together seven talks on the background to the Chernobyl accident which were given on 2 September 1986 in London to members of the Uranium Institute. The purpose of the seminar was to assist Institute members who were not themselves reactor specialists to understand the implications of the accident for the future of the nuclear industry. The Anglo-French team of speakers were all people closely concerned in their professional lives with the issues being discussed:

John Dunster   Director, British National Radiological Protection Board

Dr John Gittus   Director of Safety and Reliability, United Kingdom Atomic Energy Authority

Terence Price   Secretary-General, The Uranium Institute

Peter Saunders   Head, Environmental Impact Assessment, Harwell, UK

Dr Pierre Tanguy   Inspector-General for Nuclear Safety, Electricité de France

Dr John Wright   Corporate Director of Health and Safety, Central Electricity Generating Board, UK.

The talks and discussion are now being published so that a wider audience can benefit from the explanations of safety policy which were given in the course of the seminar.

The Uranium Institute

The Uranium Institute is an association of industrial enterprises involved with the use of uranium for the production of electricity. It currently embraces 68 organisations—electrical utilities, mining companies and fuel processors and traders—drawn from 18 nations. Its purpose is to provide a forum for the exchange and analysis of information.

Contents

Introduction to reactor physics

TERENCE PRICE

No matter how simple the language in which explanations of nuclear safety are couched, underlying them are a number of physical principles which may not be familiar to those who are not themselves directly concerned with nuclear reactors. Without some awareness of these principles, concepts which were central to the causes of the accident, such as 'positive void coefficient', are virtually incomprehensible. The purpose of this paper, therefore, is to provide the necessary background in a form which does not require any prior knowledge of nuclear physics.

Matter and its nuclear behaviour

To start at the beginning (Fig. 1): matter is composed of three main constituents—positively charged *protons*, neutral *neutrons* (with almost the same weight as protons) and the much lighter, negatively charged *electrons*. The protons and neutrons are joined together in very small and very dense nuclei, around which fly the orbital electrons, making the whole *atom* electrically neutral.

The chemical behaviour of an atom is determined entirely by the number of protons. Hydrogen has 1 proton, oxygen 8, iron 26 and uranium 92. It is possible for a given *element*—that is, a given number of protons—to be associated with more than one, indeed in many cases several, different numbers of neutrons. Thus hydrogen exists in the normal form of hydrogen with one proton, and in the much rarer form of *deuterium*, with one proton and one neutron. Chemically these different forms, or *isotopes*, behave identically. Their nuclear behaviour is, however, quite different. Hydrogen absorbs neutrons appreciably, deuterium hardly at all. Similarly uranium-235—that is uranium with 92 protons and 143 neutrons—behaves very differently from the much commoner naturally occurring isotope uranium-238 (92 protons and 146

1

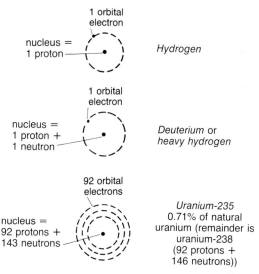

Fig. 1. Atoms and nuclei (nucleus size ~ 10^{-12} centimetres; atomic size ~ 10^{-8} centimetres)

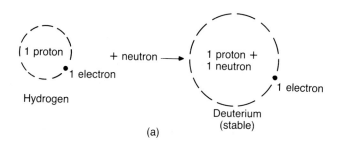

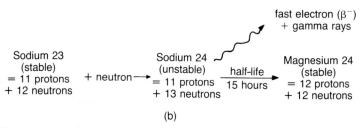

Fig. 2. Neutron absorption: (a) adding a neutron to give a stable product; (b) beta decay following neutron absorption

2

neutrons). The numbers 235 and 238 are referred to as the *mass numbers*. The number 92 for uranium is its *atomic number*.

Ninety-two elements are known in nature. With light elements, like oxygen, the normal ratio of neutrons to protons is about equal to one. For the heaviest elements—uranium being the 92nd and the heaviest—the neutron to proton ratio rises to about 1.5. This is important in determining the behaviour of the products of the fission process. For each element there is a narrow band of neutrons within which the isotope is stable, or fairly stable. Outside this range the nucleus will not hold together, and consequently is not found in nature.

One isotope can be manufactured from another in a variety of ways; but in reactors it is mainly a matter of adding neutrons, by exposing an element to a flux of neutrons. In some cases the resulting product, with a mass number or weight increased by one atomic unit, is stable. But in many cases it is not—it has too many neutrons for stability—and seeks to find stability by a process called *beta decay* (Fig. 2), in which the nucleus fires off a high-speed electron (known as a *beta particle*), and usually also some penetrating electromagnetic radiation called *gamma rays*, at the same time as one neutron disappears and is replaced by a proton. With some isotopes more than one beta decay may occur, giving a chain of daughter products.

This is what happens when a neutron is added to uranium-238. But with uranium-235 something quite different happens (Fig. 3). Instead of getting $_{92}U^{236}$ (uranium-236 with 92 protons) every time, as one might expect, in about 85% of neutron captures the nucleus splits or *fissions* into two unequal parts, the mass number of one being round about 100 units and that of the other round about 136. Two new elements are created in each fission: in the lighter portion, for instance, strontium or molybdenum; and for the heavier portion, for instance, iodine or caesium. There is a range of possible results from fission (Fig. 4), so statistically one finishes up with a collection of *fission products* grouped around these mass numbers, all chemically different from uranium. Some of these fission products are chemically capable of being taken up by the body, if they happen to get into the food chain.

If an isotope is unstable, or radioactive, its probability of disintegration per unit time is a constant which is characteristic of the particular isotope. The mathematical consequence is that the

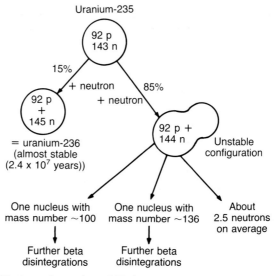

Fig. 3.   Fission of uranium-235 (p = proton, n = neutron)

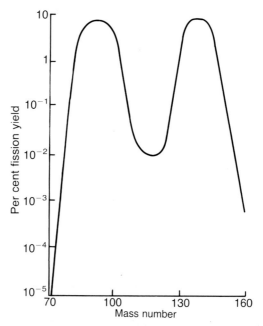

Fig. 4.   Mass yield for thermal neutron fission of uranium-235

rate of disintegration of a sample is proportional to the number of nuclei of the isotope remaining. The decay then follows what is known as an exponential law, the best known property of which is that the time needed for 50% of the nuclei to disintegrate is a constant, known as the *half-life* (Fig. 5). After one half-life the number of nuclei has dropped to 50%; after two half-lives it is down to 25%. The longer the half-life, the smaller is the intensity of the radioactivity—a point often overlooked by people who worry about long-lived nuclear waste.

The old unit of radioactive intensity was the *curie*, equal to 3.7 × 10^{10} disintegrations per second. This apparently odd choice was made because it was the number of disintegrations in one gram of radium, and was of practical importance 40 years ago to the medical profession. It is still used when very large quantities are being discussed, as at Chernobyl. For smaller quantities the unit is the very much smaller *bequerel*, equal to one disintegration per second.

Returning to the fission process: the neutron to proton ratio of the fissioning uranium nucleus is greater than that found among stable elements with about half its atomic mass. Consequently, the

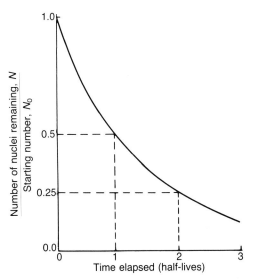

Fig. 5. Radioactive disintegration; the half-life is characteristic of the particular isotope

fission products have too many neutrons, and are mostly unstable, and they decay by beta decay until stability is restored. The process of adjustment is accompanied by some release of energy, and by the emission of beta and gamma rays. The beta particles or electrons are easily stopped by a few millimetres of solid matter. The gamma rays are more penetrating—something like a foot of concrete will reduce their intensity only by a factor of about ten. In the process of absorption both beta and gamma rays can knock the electrons off the absorbing atoms, which are then said to be *ionised*.

Ionised atoms are chemically very reactive. Specifically, if radioactive material is ingested, some of the atoms of the body can become ionised, and then join up with other atoms in ways which nature never intended. The quantity of such unwanted bio-chemical reactions depends on the total quantity of ionisation; and also on the concentration of such ionised atoms per unit of distance which the nuclear particle penetrates through matter while being stopped.

Some of the heaviest nuclei (such as the artificially produced isotope plutonium-239—see Fig. 8) disintegrate spontaneously in their search for stability by firing off not an electron, but what is known as an *alpha particle*, which is a clump of two protons and two neutrons (Fig. 6)—in fact, a helium atom minus its orbital electrons. These alpha particles are heavier and more highly charged than electrons (or beta rays), and therefore cause a much higher density of ionisation along the track before they are stopped. That is why their efficiency in causing biological damage, for a given amount of energy deposited along the track, is considerably greater than that of beta particles or gamma rays.

Nuclear reactors
Now let us go back to the fission process, and relate it to nuclear reactors. In nuclear terms a relatively large amount of energy is associated with each fission. That is the basic source of heat in a reactor. With 3×10^{16} fissions per second one has 1 megawatt of reactor heat. But equally important is the fact that there is also another by-product, which is more neutrons. Out of a fission of uranium-235 come sometimes 2, sometimes 3 neutrons, with an average yield of about 2.5. These neutrons are available to go on

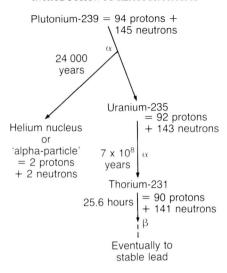

Fig. 6. Alpha decay of plutonium-239; the times given are half-lives

and induce fresh fissions in adjacent uranium-235 nuclei (Fig. 7). So the possibility of a chain reaction is immediately apparent. Incidently there is no problem about finding a neutron to start the process. They are always present in small quantities, due to cosmic rays. But in reactor start-up one can use a neutron source, to improve instrumental response and hence safety.

Not only uranium but also virtually all materials, with very few exceptions, absorb neutrons. So the reactor has to be designed in such a way that wasteful absorption in the structural materials is minimised, so as to leave one neutron available out of the ration of 2.5 to carry on the chain of fissions. That is why zirconium is used as a reactor structural material—it has relatively low neutron absorption. Steel is not intrinsically good in this respect, but it is strong enough to be used in the form of thin tubes; what one loses in one direction one gains in the other. The early Russian reactors used steel, but later on zirconium was adopted to save neutrons. The oxygen in uranium oxide ceramic fuel also has low neutron absorption—as well as permitting higher temperature operation. The chain reaction can also be promoted by artificially *enriching* the proportion of uranium-235 over the very small proportion (0.7%) found in nature.

7

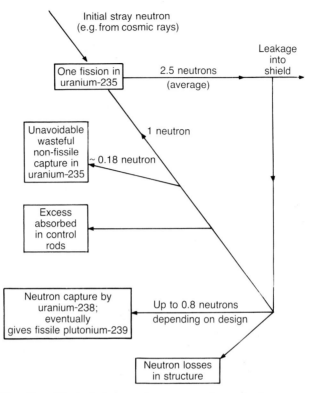

Fig. 7. Simplified chain-reaction process in typical reactor

Neutrons are most efficiently absorbed by uranium, and indeed other materials, when they are travelling slowly—much more slowly than when they are produced in the fission process. (It is a little like catching a ball—it is easier when it is travelling slowly.) Otherwise they bounce off nuclei. The neutrons can be slowed down by being bounced off nuclei, which—for reasons of mechanics—should preferably be not too much heavier than the neutrons themselves: the maximum energy loss occurs if we use hydrogen, which has the same weight as a neutron (think of billiard balls). That is why water—H_2O—is used for this purpose. Another possibility is heavy water, where the hydrogen (or deuterium) nucleus is twice as heavy (one proton, one neutron in the nucleus—mass number = 2), but still light enough for the neutron to lose a good deal of energy when bouncing off it. A third

8

option is graphite, where the nucleus is 12 times heavier than the neutron—rather heavier than one would like, but still usable for this purpose. With the relatively unimportant exception of beryllium, these are the only practical materials used for slowing down neutrons in engineering solutions. Other elements either absorb neutrons too strongly, or are structurally unsuitable.

These three materials, hydrogen, heavy hydrogen or deuterium, and graphite, are called *moderators*, presumably because they moderate the speed of the neutrons. The first two, in the form of water, can also be used as coolants, as in pressurised water reactors (PWRs) and boiling water reactors (BWRs), a category which includes Chernobyl. A graphite reactor needs a separate coolant, which then (depending on the choice) may need to be separated by tubing from the moderator: hence the tube structure of Chernobyl. But the advanced gas-cooled reactors (AGRs) use carbon dioxide, which does not need separation from graphite. Partly because the graphite is directly cooled, its temperature in the AGR is considerably lower than that at Chernobyl—which was 650–750 degrees Celcius. During normal operation about 5% of the total 3200 megawatts of heat at Chernobyl was released in the graphite, as a result of absorption of neutron energy and also of gamma radiation. In fact it ran red hot, when it was able to dissipate its heat partly by radiation to the water-cooled zirconium tubes.

After bouncing around in the moderator the neutrons eventually reach a lower speed where their energies are of the same order as those of the atoms in the crystal lattice off which they are bouncing. They are then said to be in thermal equilibrium with their surroundings, and are therefore called *thermal neutrons*. Reactors using them are called *thermal reactors*—the name actually has nothing to do with the fact that they happen to produce heat. Thermal neutrons travel slowly by nuclear standards —a mere 2.2 kilometres a second at room temperature.

One of the materials in the reactor which absorbs thermal neutrons is the second and much more common form of uranium, U238. It is not itself naturally fissile when bombarded with neutrons. However, if it absorbs a neutron it produces an unstable nucleus, uranium-239, which fairly quickly changes in a two-stage beta-decay process to a new element *plutonium*, with 94 protons and 145 neutrons, giving a mass number of 239 (Fig. 8).

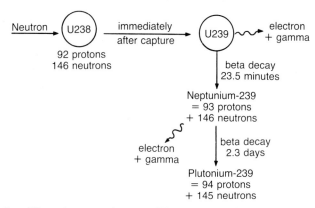

Fig. 8. *Plutonium production (U = uranium)*

Plutonium-239 does not occur naturally. Like uranium-235, it is fissionable, or *fissile*, with slow neutrons. So the neutrons lost in uranium-238 are not entirely wasted—the plutonium by-product will to some extent assist the chain reaction, given a little time.

However, if too many neutrons are absorbed in the uranium-238 there will not be that vital one neutron remaining to carry on the chain reaction. It would be like a man who invested so much of his income that he had nothing to live on, and starved. Absorption in uranium-238 therefore has to be controlled, and for physics reasons which are too complicated to go into here, this involves having fuel elements in the form of rods or plates set in a *lattice* structure. The lattice spacing in a graphite reactor is about 25 centimetres, or 10 inches. In a water reactor it is much less.

The spaces between the fuel elements are taken up mainly by the moderator and by the coolant. In a light water reactor these are one and the same thing. Where this is not so, it may be necessary to separate the coolant from the moderator. No separation is needed in a graphite reactor using carbon dioxide as coolant, like the AGRs. But the water coolant used at Chernobyl is not chemically compatible with hot graphite and is separated from it by tubing. So by a combination of physics and chemistry one is led in the two directions of *pressure vessel* reactors (like those using water both as coolant and moderator, such as the PWR type pioneered in the USA); and *pressure tube* reactors, where the coolant flows over the fuel element but is separated from the moderator—as at Chernobyl or in the Canadian CANDU reactors.

There is also a further subdivision, into *direct cycle* reactors—as at Chernobyl—where the coolant water passes through the reactor and the resulting steam goes directly into the turbine; and *indirect cycle* systems, where there is an intermediate heat exchanger. The former have some thermodynamic advantages. The disadvantage is that in normal operation one has to accept that the turbine uses slightly radioactive steam; and of course under fault conditions one could have more severe problems; whereas with the indirect cycle the radioactivity is contained within the reactor shielding.

Whatever system is chosen, an arrangement is needed which will ensure that one neutron is left to create a new fission in uranium-235 for every uranium-235 nucleus which was fissioned in the first place (Fig. 9). In practice this number needs to be a little greater than one, to give a margin for control—for instance because the neutron balance is affected by temperature for a variety of physical and nuclear reasons. Moreover, in order to have a practical machine capable of burning up sufficient amounts of uranium, the effect of depletion of the fuel also has to be taken into account. So some *excess reactivity* needs to be available. In the example (Fig. 9) it is $1.02 - 1 = 0.02$.

An important source of neutron loss is leakage out of the reactor into the surrounding shielding. For purely geometrical reasons, the proportion of neutrons leaking out of the reactor core decreases as the size of the reactor increases. Again for purely geometrical reasons, leakage is least when the core shape approximates to a sphere. In practice one cannot easily use a sphere in engineering solutions, and one has to accept a cylinder as a reasonable approximation. The Chernobyl core was 12 metres in diameter and 7 metres high.

This leads to the concept of *critical size*. If the reactor is too small, the chain reaction cannot continue—there is too much leakage. If it is made larger, eventually the leakage becomes sufficiently unimportant and allows the chain reaction to propagate. If the reactor is made still larger, then it might be possible for part of the core to become critical while another part is effectively shut down. In very large cores there is therefore a potential spatial stability problem which the control system must deal with. This was a design and operational consideration in the large Chernobyl reactor.

The leakage has one other effect: the *flux* of neutrons (defined

11

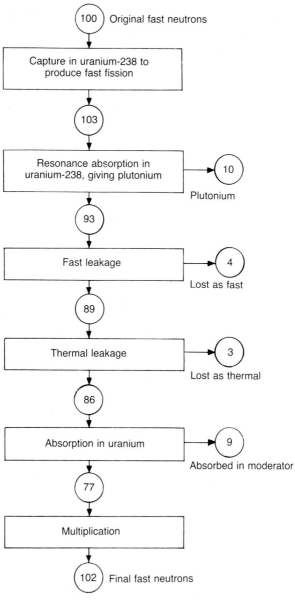

Fig. 9. Chain reaction with positive reactivity (not counting losses in control rods); from Murray R. L., Introduction to Nuclear Engineering, George Allen & Unwin

as their density times their velocity) has a maximum at the centre of the reactor and decreases towards the edges. This means that the heat production in the reactor, which comes from neutron-induced fissions, is not uniform (Fig. 10). This in turn means that the heat transfer has to be regulated so that conditions are safe at the hottest spot. The problem is reduced as far as possible by using a combination of absorbers and fuel design to 'flatten' the flux across the middle of the core.

The *control rods* are made of materials which absorb neutrons strongly—like cadmium or boron. If they are pushed into the core—a reactor 'scram' in operators' jargon—the reactor is shut down. In normal operation they are adjusted so that over the reactor core, at any given time, there is exactly one neutron causing fission per neutron that caused fission in the previous generation.

The balancing out of the excess reactivity must be very precise, because the speed with which each neutron generation succeeds another is very rapid, around one ten-thousandth of a second per generation. So in a single second thousands of generations could succeed each other. Even slight imbalances would then become significant. If these were the only principles at work, an excess reactivity of only 0.01 would give a 100-fold power increase in $\frac{1}{10}$ second! In fact reactors can be controlled for practical purposes only because of the fortuitous existence of another phenomenon—*delayed neutrons*. Not all the 2.5 neutrons (on average) are released exactly at the moment of fission. A small fraction—about ¾% in uranium-235, rather less in plutonium—come from disintegrating neutron-rich fission products and are delayed by

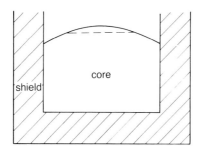

Fig. 10.   Distribution of heat production and neutron flux across core; dashed line shows case of power flattening

between $\frac{1}{20}$ second and up to 55 seconds. The average delayed fraction with the Chernobyl fuel was about $\frac{1}{2}\%$.

By keeping the reactivity balance such that the chain reaction can continue to propagate only with the aid of these delayed neutrons, it is possible to regulate the reactor so that the power grows so slowly as to be easily controllable in normal operation. Nothing must be allowed to bring the reactor up to a condition where criticality—that is, the continuation of the chain reaction—can occur on the basis of the non-delayed neutrons only. It is vital that absorbing materials should not be capable of being withdrawn from the reactor quickly and on a scale which will threaten an approach to what is called *prompt criticality*—criticality on the basis of the non-delayed neutrons. According to the Russian analysis, in its final moments the Chernobyl reactor came to prompt criticality, with power rising by a factor of 10, possibly 100, in a second or so. In 4 seconds it was all over and the reactor in ruins—bearing out Enrico Fermi's saying in 1942 that without delayed neutrons there would be no nuclear power.

The ability of the control rods to deal with the fluctuations in reactivity which can occur in normal operation needs to be considered very carefully. There is a variety of means through which the temperature of the reactor can affect the reactivity. The change in the density of water with temperature is an obvious cause. There are also nuclear causes. The neutrons are approximately in thermal equilibrium with their surroundings: that determines their speed, which as mentioned affects the ease with which they are captured by the various components of the reactor. The variation of capture probability (or *cross-section*) with speed is in fact quite complicated (Fig. 11). Moreover the neutrons do not have just one speed, but a spectrum, all the way down from the high speed at their birth to a peak corresponding with thermal equilibrium. The vibrations of the atoms in the lattice also play a part. They get faster as the temperature goes up—that is what temperature is—and it will seem to the neutrons as though they are approaching or receding more quickly, so changing the capture probability. The upshot of all this is that there is a variety of temperature coefficients of reactivity. At Chernobyl there was a negative coefficient with respect to the fuel temperature. That would give a little help towards shutting the reactor down if the power started running away. The graphite temperature contrib-

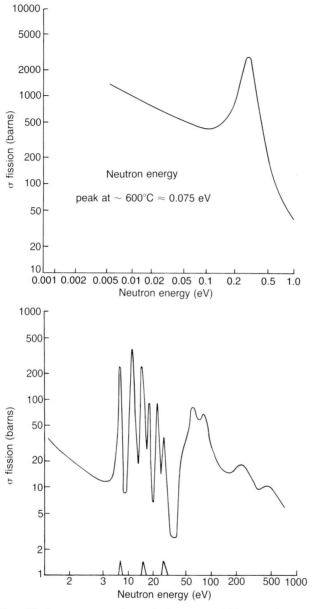

Fig. 11. Fission cross-section of plutonium-239 as a function of neutron energy (1 barn = 10^{-24} square centimetres)

15

uted a positive coefficient. Most importantly, the steam voidage contributed a significant positive coefficient, making for instability, of 2×10^{-4} per volume per cent of steam. At the top of this boiling water reactor the design intention was to run with 14% of steam. As the delayed neutron fraction is 5×10^{-3} (½%) the effect of the steam void coefficient is far from negligible. It is a major source of instability in the Soviet RBMK reactors, and played a major role in the accident, as an unfortunate result of operator errors which greatly changed the hydraulic conditions affecting the conversion of water into steam.

To control this intrinsically rather unstable reactor there was an array of 211 control rods, which followed the indications of various sensors distributed around the reactor. As in any reactor, their efficiency as a control system depended on having enough of them positioned within the reactor, at places where a slight movement could make a large change in the number of neutrons absorbed (i.e. in positions where the neutron flux gradient was large). Having control rods in the core does of course mean wasting neutrons; but the control requirement is overriding. The USSR had rigid rules requiring sufficient rods to be left in the core to deal with anticipated reactivity changes. These rules were disregarded.

Fission products
There are some important points concerning the fission products. The fact that they continue to disintegrate, in an effort to achieve a stable neutron–proton balance, means that some energy release will continue after the reactor is shut down, for as long as this process continues. In other words, one cannot totally shut off the heat production from a reactor. Fission product heating turns out to be a highly significant safety consideration (Table 1). If a chain reaction is stopped completely by the control rods being pushed in, then one minute later a reactor rated in operation at 1000 megawatts electrical—which means 3000 megawatts of heat—will still be generating 100 megawatts from residual fission product heating. After one day it will be 19 megawatts. Even one month later the heat output will be 7 megawatts. With such heat release, the temperature of even a massive reactor structure could rise disturbingly quickly, if for any fault reason there were no cooling—possibly by hundreds of degrees Celsius per day. So the *guaranteed* provision of an emergency core cooling system is a

Table 1.   *Fission product shutdown heating at Chernobyl*

	Megawatts
Heat production in operation	3200
Time after shutdown	
1 second	192
1 hour	64
1 day	19
1 week	12
1 month	7
1 year	1–2

fundamental necessity in all except the lowest-powered reactors. Hence also the anxiety in the days immediately after the Chernobyl accident lest the whole structure might melt, and fall into a pond which happened to be underneath, causing a chemical explosion. That danger is now past; and the Soviets have installed a cooling system to keep the bottom of the reactor structure at an acceptable temperature.

There is one other phenomenon associated with the decay of fission products which is of major relevance to the analysis of Chernobyl. There is one fission product decay chain (Fig. 12) which produces a very strong neutron absorber, xenon-135. While the reactor is operating the xenon reacts with neutrons, and is itself destroyed in the process, about as fast as it is created. This has the effect of wasting neutrons, and to that extent one has to build extra reactivity into the core; but it is taken into account in the design and does not stop the reactor operating. However, once

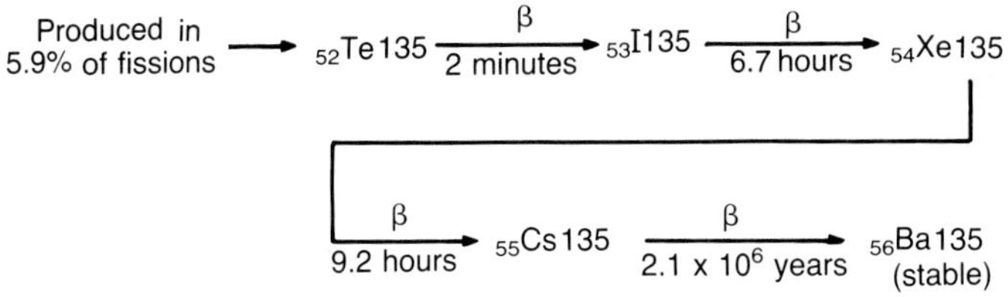

Fig. 12. Production and decay of xenon-135 'poison' (Te = tellurium, I = iodine, Xe = xenon, Cs = caesium, Ba = barium)

17

the reactor is shut down the xenon is no longer being destroyed, and can build up to a maximum value in a time determined by the half-lives involved. The maximum of this additional source of neutron absorption, or *'poisoning'*, occurs about 10.4 hours after shutdown. It can have the effect of making it impossible to restart a reactor until the xenon has decayed away, which would take around 2 days.

This phenomenon played a part in the Chernobyl disaster. A planned experiment involving power reduction was interrupted by a decision to keep the reactor on load for grid operational reasons, though at somewhat reduced power; and power was later reduced still further. The result was that there was some build-up of xenon, which to keep the reactor operating meant going into a control rod regime where most of the rods were out of the reactor, and incapable of being brought back in less than about 6 seconds. So the reactor was in a potentially dangerous state. This was not the sole cause of the disaster, but it was an important contributor.

Poison

For completeness I should also mention one other use of the word 'poison' in reactor engineering. As the uranium is used up, the reactivity falls; and the heat distribution also changes, because the uranium tends to be used faster in the middle of the reactor due to the spatial distribution of the neutron density. This has to be taken into account when designing the control sysytem. One can minimise the effects on reactivity, and hence on the control system, by introducing a neutron absorber—a *burnable poison*— deliberately: as the uranium is used up so is the poison, making the reactivity changes during the core lifetime smaller, and reducing control problems. Whether this is done or not is a matter of economics. Every neutron lost costs money: but so does a shutdown period. It is a simple matter of a trade-off, one against the other.

Conclusion

These are the principles involved in the design of any thermal reactor. There is perhaps an analogy to be made with aircraft design. Aircraft can be very different: a Boeing 747 and a small Cessna seem to be worlds apart. But the principles remain very similar. It is much the same with reactors.

What happened at Chernobyl

JOHN GITTUS

The Chernobyl reactor went wrong because it had three design deficiencies: instability, slow shutdown and inadequate automation of safety systems. Coupled with maloperation during an experiment by the staff, these deficiencies led to the accident. The Russians acknowledge the deficiencies and have described sweeping design changes which they are making to put matters right.

What happened at Chernobyl is that the uranium fuel in the nuclear reactor overheated, and it consequently gave off radioactive fumes (my description of particulate and aerosol emissions), which were carried by the wind to places 100 miles away and more, contaminating land and buildings. Thirty-one people, most of them firemen and other emergency workers, have since died. The majority of these people who died were 'acute fatalities', or early deaths. They were people who received intense radiation from the cloud of activity, and indeed some of them were probably exposed to direct radiation from the reactor core.

How it happened

To answer the question of how it happened involves giving an explanation of the experiment which the reactor operators were performing at Chernobyl. The experiment went wrong, and that was the cause of the accident. Figure 1 illustrates, in the most elementary form, the concept of the experiment. The thing that looks like a propeller is a representation of a turbine. The turbine at the nuclear power station operates the alternator, which generates electricity. They were doing an experiment in which they were using a turbine to power a pump. I have represented that process by putting the pump on the shaft of the turbine. In actual fact the pump was driven by an electric motor, the motor

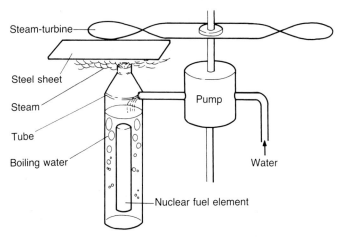

Fig. 1. Concept of the Chernobyl experiment

was energised by electricity from the alternator, and the alternator driven by the turbine.

The turbine is being rotated by a jet of steam. As it revolves, like a child's propeller, it rotates the pump which is pumping water into the tube. The reactor is a pressure tube reactor; the tube is one of the pressure tubes containing the nuclear fuel elements. In its behaviour and construction, the fuel element is like an immersion heater or a heating element in a kettle. There is an outer cladding tube, and inside there is a ceramic. In the case of the Chernobyl reactor that ceramic is uranium dioxide; and in the case of an electric kettle it is alumina. The only real difference is that there is a heating wire right up the centre of the alumina in the electric kettle, which is what boils the water. In the case of the reactor, the water is being boiled by the heat given off when atoms of uranium are fissioned. The fuel element spontaneously gives off heat, which boils the water, which produces the steam, which blows the turbine round, which drives the pump, which sucks in water and cascades it into the tube in quantities just sufficient to replace the water that has been boiled away. It is as though the electric kettle was put under a tap, and water was dribbled in at a speed that just kept pace with the rate at which it was being boiled away.

The experiment, in this simplified representation, consisted of placing a sheet of steel in the path of the jet of steam so that it no longer drove the turbine. The turbine then free-wheeled. It still kept pumping water, but it gradually slowed down. So the amount of water gradually diminished, while the amount that was being boiled away was constant: the amount of heat being given off by the fuel element unfortunately was not reduced, even though it should have been reduced automatically. If the automatic system had failed, or been turned off—and the operators had turned it off—then the operators should have manually switched off the heat that was being generated by the fuel element. Otherwise, as anyone can see, in time the pump will stop pumping water, the 'kettle' will boil dry, and the element will 'burn out' (the very terminology that is used in talking about electric kettles transfers directly to the nuclear case). The element in the reactor happens to be loaded with volatile radioactive substances, caesium and iodine in particular. When it heats up to red heat—being no longer surrounded by boiling water—these volatile substances will come off as a vapour, and instead of steam coming out there will be clouds of radioactive vapours.

That in a very simple form is exactly what happened at Chernobyl. The operators diverted steam from the turbine. The rate at which the primary coolant pumps were operating gradually diminished, to a point where insufficient cooling was being produced in the pressure tubes or channels. Accordingly, the volume of steam increased. In this conceptual explanation, what would then happen is that the level of water would go down, to a point where the fuel was no longer adequately cooled; and so its temperature would go up.

I can add some technical details, still within the scope of this illustration, to explain two other matters that have been mentioned. One is the *positive void coefficient*. The 'void' is the space in the tube which does not have water in; it contains steam, but in reactor parlance it is a void. As the water level boiled down, so the size of this void increased. Now it is a property of a reactor of this type that as the void grows larger, the heat that is being given off by the fuel element will tend to increase. It is not only that the element gets hotter because it no longer has any water round the top part of it: in addition to that, there is more heat to take away; and less water to take it away. That is the effect of the positive void coefficient: a positive increase in heat produced as the void gets bigger, because the number of neutrons absorbed by water diminishes.

The second term is *prompt criticality*. This happens when the chain reaction no longer needs the delayed neutrons (see page 13) in order to maintain it. Normally, both the delayed neutrons and the prompt neutrons that come from the fission are used to keep the chain reaction going. But if the reactivity rises—and it rose here because of the positive void coefficient—to a level at which the delayed neutrons are no longer needed, then the time interval for doubling the neutron population, and hence the power, comes down to a very brief period—a fraction of a second.

So what happened in the Chernobyl accident is that the power increased in two stages. The first stage was a slow increase, due to the positive void coefficient. This would appear to take its time from the rate at which the water level was going down (it is in fact more complicated, but this is the simple explanation). As soon as the conditions in the reactor were such that the delayed neutrons were no longer needed to keep the nuclear reaction going, the reactor went prompt critical. The time for doubling the power was then less than a second. The power went rocketing up until the ceramic pellets shattered. It was this shattering process which distributed the fuel and so contributed towards the shutting down of the chain reaction. Indeed, there is still some controversy about exactly what it was that terminated the chain reaction; but the balance of Russian opinion was behind the explanation that I have just given.

What happened next was that 8 tonnes of the 140 tonnes of fuel were ejected from the reactor. Piles of debris, fuel and graphite were deposited on the ground near the reactor. Caesium and iodine vapours were given off. Plutonium was present in the fuel particles. It might also have been given off in larger quantities from the overheated fuel if the temperature had risen to a high enough level; but this did not happen. As for the consequences, John Dunster will speak about these, and I shall only include a few remarks.

The authorities evacuated 135 000 people who lived within 30 kilometres of the site. In this way they successfully limited the radiation dose which most of those people received, to levels which might be comparable with those which would be attained by radiation workers in a lifetime's work under modern circumstances. So for these people the doses were not dramatically high. For people living only a few kilometres away from the plant, the difference between their life expectation, or the likelihood of their getting cancer, compared with those of people who were remote from the accident, would probably be considerably less than the difference between those who smoke cigarettes habitually and those who do not. So although some harm has certainly been suffered, it is not going to have a dramatic impact on the death rate in that community or upon the remainder of their lives. The people close in received far heavier doses of radiation; they were the 31 early fatalities.

The Russians are clearing up and decontaminating. We have been running computer models to try and predict the outcome, and have concluded that they should probably be able to get the land back into limited economic use, except immediately round the plant, by next year. That is indeed what the Russian delegation confirmed in Vienna.

The reactor
I have rather oversimplified the description of the reactor in describing the accident and I will now give a little more detail. In an RBMK reactor there is the graphite moderator (Fig. 2) which

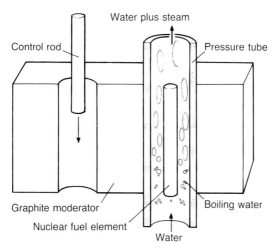

Fig. 2. Russian RBMK reactor core

slows the fast neutrons down to the relatively low speeds at which they can easily fission uranium atoms. Uranium atoms are present in uranium dioxide in the fuel element. Water is injected by the pump at the bottom of the pressure tube. It boils as it goes up, and what comes out is actually boiling water and not, as I said earlier, steam—that was one of my simplifications. The boiling water goes to a steam-separating drum, where the steam rises to the top, and is taken off to the turbine; the water remains at the bottom and is pumped back into the channel. Although I did not show this in Fig. 1, it is the same water going round all the time. It is condensed after it has gone through the turbine or collected in the steam separator and used again. I mentioned that the operators should have switched off the heat from the fuel element. That can be done by means of a neutron absorber—a control rod or shutdown rod—which can be pulled out to increase the power or pushed in to reduce the power. If it is pushed in far enough it absorbs effectively all the neutrons, so that heat is no longer given out by the fuel element.

In the accident this should have happened automatically. The moment the operators approached danger the automatic safety system should have made the control rods go into the reactor and stop heat production. This would be like switching off the kettle automatically, as happens with a modern kettle. The same should occur with reactors: if boiling goes beyond a certain point, an automatic signal should drop in the control rods and switch off the generation of heat. But the operators had inhibited that function, so that it could not work. They had a red button called AZ5 which they should have pressed; but they did not. They just watched the experiment going ahead, as if hypnotised, until finally the reactor began to overheat. They then pressed button AZ5; but it was far too late. The reactor was already on the rising curve due to the positive void coefficient. Within a second or so it was on the even more steep curve due to prompt criticality. The fuel disintegrated, and there was a steam explosion due to particles of fuel interacting with the water in the channels. According to the Russians, all of the nearly 2000 tubes in the reactor were burst by the steam pressure. The steam pressure went on to lift the reactor top (rather like an enormous saucepan with a lid on top), cracked it and toppled some structures that were on top of it, and the whole reactor was then exposed to the air. Fumes (radioactive aerosols) were free to move into the atmosphere, air got to the graphite and set it on fire, and the zirconium tubes burned in the very hot steam, and gave off hydrogen. In addition, carbon monoxide was produced from the graphite. Both gases are inflammable and they burned or exploded as well. So a whole range of events like that took place once the accident had started.

The issues raised by Chernobyl

PIERRE TANGUY

The list of key points given in Table 1 was prepared in early June 1986 when we had to explain about Chernobyl to the people in France and in some international meetings, at a time when we knew very little about the accident. The main technical information came from Mr Gorbachov's speech, in rather general terms. He was the first to talk about the 'power surge'. People could not accept that we in France should do nothing; at least we had to confirm that there were lessons to be learned from the accident. It was quite clear that human factors had been the determining cause. In Vienna in August 1986 we got evidence that this was even more the case than we had expected.

John Gittus has described the experiment being conducted just before the accident; and John Wright emphasises that we in the West would certainly not authorise such an experiment in a power-producing reactor without very exceptional authorisation procedures, following a full analysis etc. The so-called 'operator errors' are mainly violations of regulations—such as deliberately shutting-off very important safety systems. At Chernobyl, starting with the superintendent of the plant down to the operator in the control room—and maybe going even higher, at the Soviet Ministry of Power and Electrification, or even in the safety commissions—there was not a proper awareness of nuclear risk. In view of all the regulatory violations performed by the operators, one might almost think that it was malicious sabotage. Indeed, in some ways that might have been a more satisfactory explanation. In reality the situation was even worse. The operators appeared to be operating a reactor quite well, in the sense that they had very high operational availability. They were convinced that the design was good. But they were not aware of how a reactivity accident might occur. That much is obvious. The operators were also

Table 1. Initial safety lessons learnt from Chernobyl (list prepared in June 1986, six weeks after the accident)

- Importance of the human factor

    At every level, from top management to plant operators, all must be aware of severe accident risks

- Need to understand the accident's specific causes

    Requires the relevant technical information to be provided by the USSR

- Management of a severe accident

    Implementation of special emergency procedures
    Operator training for severe accidents
    Containment behaviour under extreme conditions
    Use of remote technology in highly radioactive environment
    Off-site emergency preparedness

- Strengthening international co-operation

    Agreements on information and assistance
    IAEA's role in incident reporting and safety review
    Radiological action levels

- Impact on public opinion

    Nuclear energy risks versus benefits
    Local discussions on consequences of severe accidents

probably not informed about the elementary physics of xenon poisoning, which played a very important role in the events. It seems that when the operator finally pushed the red button, it was because he felt that the test was over; three seconds later there was an explosion.

The second issue (Table 1) was that in June 1986 we had a conviction that this accident was directly related to the characteristics of the Soviet RBMK. At that time we did not have all the necessary information, so we had to be cautious. But it was already clear that this type of event could not take place in any of the Western reactors. We got all the necessary information at Vienna in August, and it confirmed that we were right. In June we had to tell journalists and policy-makers that there were some lessons to be learned from the accident. The lessons did not involve going back to our own design—we could not see how to improve it—but rather looking at severe accidents, which Chernobyl certainly was. We needed to look at the five items listed in Table 1—which are exactly the same items which were learned from Three Mile Island. There is in fact nothing radically new for us coming out of Chernobyl; but the Soviets may have learned some new lessons, very painfully.

There are of course conclusions to be drawn on international protection and safety. There is no doubt that plant safety can be improved by bilateral co-operation between technical people, though how far an administrative structure like the International Atomic Energy Agency can assist is uncertain. Finding ways of improving co-operation efficiently is not easy; but what is not in question is the absolute political necessity of expanding the role of the IAEA.

Now about public opinion. In France, at least until the fall-out from Chernobyl, people did not worry too much about the accident, or about the possibility of such an accident happening in France. Chernobyl was far away in the Ukraine, and anyway life itself is dangerous. But when they were told that their own salad would be dangerous; that they should not let their children play in the open air; and that if a woman was pregnant she should consider the possibility of abortion—and all this because of something that took place far away—suddenly they had the feeling that nuclear energy simply could not be tolerated. They could not accept the idea that, even though they were living far away from a dangerous installation, all of a sudden their private lives and the lives of their children could be affected. The result was that polls showed that the support for nuclear power in France fell by about 15 points after Chernobyl. France had been very pro-nuclear— roughly 65:35 in favour of nuclear. This changed to 50:50; and what is more important is that the 15 percentage points were lost among people who are not the type who demonstrate in the streets against nuclear war. It was mainly women and older members of the community. Regaining their confidence will not be easy, but is probably necessary if the nuclear programme is to continue.

After the accident

Figure 1 is a sketch of the Chernobyl nuclear plant. Figure 2, showing how it was after the accident, gives an idea of the scale of the explosion. The debris was highly radioactive, and even five months after the accident, in September 1986, workers could not go closer than 200 metres to the damaged building, which was still leaking about 4×10^{11} bequerels of radioactive products per day. A first priority for the Russians was to isolate the radioactive source by building the structure, shown in outline, known as the 'sarcophagus' around the damaged unit. It was not an easy job, as the dose rate was very high. But without it, there could be no serious hope of bringing back people to the evacuated area, because there would still be some radioactive release from the plant and therefore some risk of contamination.

Perhaps the most important information obtained in August 1986 from the Russians was that they had shut down some or all of the RBMKs—the Chernobyl type—to introduce safety modifications to the design. For the first time they seemed to be ready to recognise that modifications were needed for safety. The modifications involve control improvements and attention to the man–machine interface.

Safety lessons

I come now to what I think are the safety lessons. First (and this must be emphasised), there is nothing totally new in the Chernobyl accident. The possibility of a reactivity accident, perhaps reaching prompt criticality, was identified 30 years ago. There were experiments in the USA in the 1950s, and an accident to a research reactor in Canada about the same time. The possibilities of reactivity insertion and of power excursions are well known. But we should not forget one issue. When we look at safety we no longer need to try to imagine new phenomena; but we must verify that already well identified risks are properly taken into account.

The second point concerns 'safety culture'—a phrase used by Dr Edmondson at Vienna, and a very good one. It is wider than simply human factors in the normal sense. Safety, not only in theory, but also in practice, is the first priority for everybody involved in the nuclear industry, from the top manager realising that safety comes before electricity production or the time taken

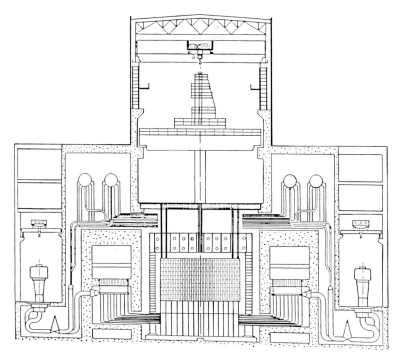

Fig. 1.   The Chernobyl plant before the accident

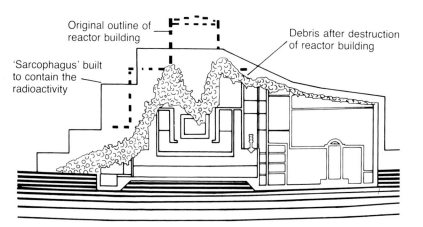

Fig. 2.   The scale of the damage to the Chernobyl plant

for shutdown etc., down to the operator. This has many implications for safety culture, which obviously did not work very well in the USSR. One is training for accident prevention. We did not get any information on whether the operators were trained using simulators to reproduce the sequences of some possible severe accidents; but obviously they did not understand the very complex operation of the plant in the actual conditions at the time of the experiment. There is also the need for permanent 'auditing' to verify that there is no routine or procedure that could cause an accident.

The third is more difficult to explain. In a good plant which is operating well—which was the case of Chernobyl in normal operation—the people may have been instructed about severe accidents, but their day-to-day experience is completely the opposite. It is very difficult to make them understand that this daily experience could give them a false impression; so we have to do some 'sensitisation'—starting with their own experience, and analysing with their participation how in some cases things could have gone wrong, and led to a severe accident. We have to demonstrate to them how their own daily experience is not inconsistent with the possibility of a severe accident.

The third lesson, therefore, is the need for defence in depth in the design. Obviously this was unsatisfactory in the Soviet RBMKs. When there is an inherent instability (and this cannot always be avoided) we have to use foresight and design the correct regulatory systems. The first step towards acceptable control is to restore stability. The second is to have an automatic shutdown system. A Canadian representative told the Vienna conference that after the accident to the NRX reactor in the 1950s the conclusion was that a shutdown system is needed which is both strong and fast: strong enough to introduce negative reactivity to cover any conceivable circumstances, and fast to operate as quickly as possible. The Russian shutdown system was neither strong nor fast. Finally, one must examine the possibility of an ultimate passive barrier to contain most of the radioactivity. Without this type of barrier, one is very dependent on the safety prevention system, and needs to ask for a very strong guarantee that its design is foolproof before accepting it.

In the case of fast breeders we have the same problem of inherent instability. So we have specified a control system which uses a lot of diverse signals to act in sufficient time. We also need a shutdown system with diversified back-up, and a containment structure able to contend with radioactivity.

In the RBMK a key factor is the amount of excess reactivity, measured in terms of equivalent control rods still inserted in the reactor. At some point one comes to a boundary, or threshold, between having a reactor that can still be controlled, and what the Russians had at the end: a reactor which was uncontrollable. In such a case the control room must have a very clear indication of where that threshold lies, in exactly the same way as in the pressurised water reactor we need a signal to tell us how far we are from boiling in the core.

Nuclear power plants are in some cases very complicated machines, difficult to operate. If they become too complicated it is a little like asking the operator to play a game by using his right hand to draw a vertical line and his left hand to draw a horizontal line. With training he may be able to draw a beautiful bird; but it is better to ask a computer to do the job, because it can do so easily. For the same reason automation should be a requirement in cases of reactors which are difficult to control. This is one of the lessons which could also apply to some Western reactors.

Unanswered questions
We got a lot of information from the Russians at Vienna in August 1986, four months after the accident, even though they were somewhat embarrassed. But there were a lot of questions which were not answered, either because the Russians did not want to answer, or because they did not have an answer, or because it would take some months, maybe years, to produce one. These questions should not be forgotten. For instance, what happened during the first 3 seconds of the power surge? Up to then we nearly understand what took place; after that point the sequence of events is still not very clear. Clarification is important, not only because it would improve our safety knowledge, but also because it would help us to know from that analysis whether a containment building could have been provided for the RBMK. This is still an open question. The Russians answered that even if there had been a containment building around the reactor it would not have contained the reactivity—it would have exploded. That may be true, but from the data we have so far been given that conclusion is

not obvious. If we are able in a fast breeder to contain very significant mechanical energy from a hypothetical accident, I should be surprised if this was impossible in an RBMK. We need to understand better the mechanisms of the radioactivity release, which were very complex, and also important for our safety knowledge. We also have no information on the accident management on site. The Russians had a unique experience, which could be of great importance to a company like Electricité de France, which has several units on the same site. The way in which they were able to shut down the other units, and then keep them in a safe state despite the highly radioactive environment, could well be of value to us. Lastly, we should very much like to have some information on the experience of decontaminating the site.

The safety of gas-cooled reactors

JOHN WRIGHT

This paper provides a simplified overview of the safety of gas-cooled reactors by looking at the safety of the early British Magnox stations. Figure 1 shows a schematic view of a steel pressure vessel Magnox reactor, together with some important typical design parameters. The reactor is contained within a steel pressure vessel. CO_2 coolant flows over natural uranium fuel housed in approximately 4000 channels within a graphite moderator, then passes via large ducts to drum boilers and gas circulators. The figure also shows the safety limits concerned with oxidation of graphite and melting of the Magnox cans.

As in other types of nuclear reactor, the effect on reactivity of changing parameters such as fuel and moderator temperatures is an important consideration. Table 1 provides this information for Magnox reactors, together with the equivalent values for PWRs and the Russian RBMKs for comparison. Advanced gas-cooled reactors (AGRs) behave similarly to Magnox reactors. The effect of reactor coolant water density, which was fundamental to the Chernobyl accident, is not relevant in the case of gas-cooled reactors. Although increasing the temperature of the graphite moderator does provide positive feedback, the timescale is sufficiently slow—typically tens of minutes—that control systems can easily counteract the effect.

Protection systems

Although the design is carefully considered to minimise the likelihood of potential faults, a highly reliable protection system is provided to shut down the reactor automatically before fuel integrity is threatened in the event of a fault developing. Table 2 shows the sensor measurements used in such a protection system. Some directly detect the fault itself (e.g. reduction of circulator

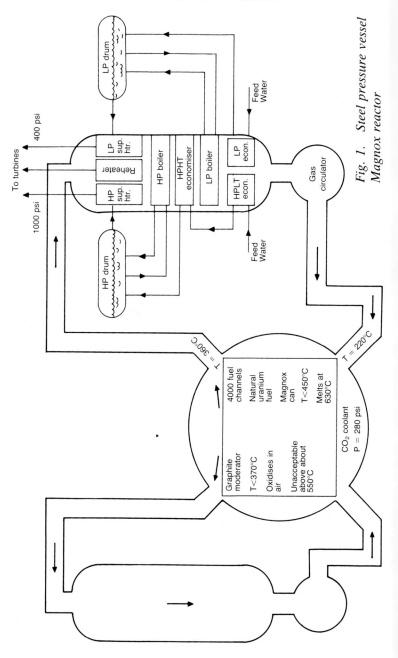

Fig. 1. Steel pressure vessel Magnox reactor

Table 1. *Effects of temperature and density changes on reactivity (values quoted are mN/% power change)*

	Response time	Reactor type		
		Magnox/AGR	PWR	RBMK
Fuel temperature	Few seconds	−4	−10	−5
Water density	Few seconds	–	−4	+10
Graphite temperature	Tens of minutes	+7	–	+25

1 mN corresponds to a reactivity of 10^{-5}.

Table 2. *Reactor protection for Magnox reactors: monitoring of reactor condition*

Direct

Rate of change of circulator speed
Rate of change of pressure
Loss of feed pressure
High gas pressure

Indirect

Neutron flux
Fuel element temperature   } Rate of change and top stop
Gas outlet temperature

speed), while others do so indirectly, by detecting the effect of a fault on the reactor. Table 3 lists the main categories of faults and shows the kinds of measurements that provide protection against each category.

Every reactor has several of each type of detector, and these are arranged in a logic system which provides redundancy (more than the minimum necessary) and diversity (more than one type or location). If something goes wrong with one of the protection systems, a further system is still able to provide protection.

Table 3.   Protection against possible faults in Magnox reactors

Fault	Protection
Depressurisation	Rate of change of pressure Fuel element temperature channel gas outlet temperature
Loss of circulators	Rate of change of circulator speed Fuel element temperature
Whole core increase in reactivity	Flux Fuel element temperature
Local increase in reactivity	Fuel element temperature Channel gas outlet temperature
Loss of feed	Low feed pressure
Over-pressurisation	High pressure

As an example, let us consider a reactivity fault, the type of fault that caused the Chernobyl release. Suppose the reactor was operating at reduced power, as was Chernobyl, and that the operator wished to increase power, for example, from 30% to 50% power. He would initially do this by pulling out control rods. The maximum rate at which this can be done in Magnox reactors is fixed by design, to limit the consequences of inadvertent withdrawal. However, suppose that the increase in power is for some reason not terminated at the point intended. What would then happen is that the measured reactor power would increase, and with it the measured fuel element temperature. The trip levels derived from these measurements are automatically set just above their current level, to give protection against any sudden changes. However, in our example, as the power and temperature increase, the trip levels can, by design, only increase relatively slowly. The temperature or other reactor characteristic being monitored therefore gradually approaches the trip level, and, when this is reached, the protection system causes all the control rods to fall into the reactor under gravity. (The control rods act much more quickly than at Chernobyl, where the shutdown rods took several seconds to become effective as they were inserted by electrically

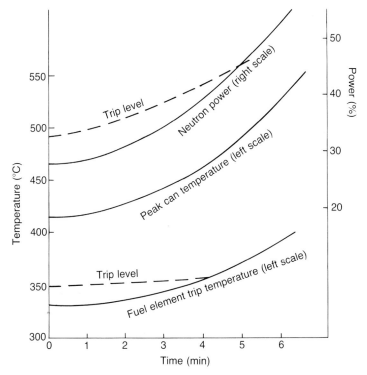

Fig. 2. Fast reactivity fault in Magnox reactor starting from 30% power

driven motors.) Figure 2 shows an example of such a fault. Recalling that Magnox cans melt at around 630°C, it can be seen that measurements of neutron power and fuel element temperature both give protection to the reactor against this fault. For other types of fault the situation is similar.

Depressurisation faults
For faults where the pressure circuit remains intact, the chance of a significant release is negligible, as the pressure circuit provides a second barrier to a release (the Magnox fuel can provides the first). Depressurisation faults could potentially pose a greater risk. Not only is a direct release path to the atmosphere then prevented only by the fuel can, but reactor cooling is more difficult as the coolant

is at reduced pressure, and there is also the potential for air to enter the reactor and produce additional heat by reacting chemically with the graphite. While the immediate concern is to prevent fuel melting, there would also be the longer-term concerns related to the possibility of a graphite fire, and the addition of reactivity due to the increasing moderator temperature.

The initial protection against such faults is from the protection system which detects the loss of pressure and the increase in temperature, together with a group of special control rods which are automatically released by pressure-sensitive switches. There are also emergency shutdown devices which enable boron balls to be fed into the reactor (boron is a good neutron absorber). In addition to all of these it is possible, as a last resort, to inject boron dust, which will stick to the fuel and graphite and keep the reactor shut down. However, having done that we have written off the reactor, as the boron cannot be removed.

Having prevented the fuel from melting within the first few minutes after a depressurisation fault, it is necessary to continue to keep temperatures under control despite the existence of reactor decay heat (see page 16). To do this we must always have some gas circulators working and the corresponding boilers fed with water, even if the connection to the grid has been lost through some simultaneous failure. Electrical supplies provided by emergency diesel generators or gas turbines are therefore provided. We also assume that some of the circulators and boilers might fail to function. An example of the reactor temperatures during such a fault with minimum cooling is shown as curve 1 of Fig. 3. There are, however, other things that can be done to reduce temperatures. If normal circulator supplies can be restored, then the circulators can be run at a higher speed. The effect of running at full speed for 90 minutes is shown as curve 2 of Fig. 3.

Both the above cases assume that the reactor is full of air instead of the normal carbon dioxide. The heat input from the chemical reaction of air with graphite can be quenched by injecting CO_2. The effect of beginning this operation after 2 hours can be seen as curve 3 of Fig. 3.

This very brief summary illustrates how the reactor is protected in depth against depressurisation faults, in terms of both initial shutdown and longer-term cooling requirements.

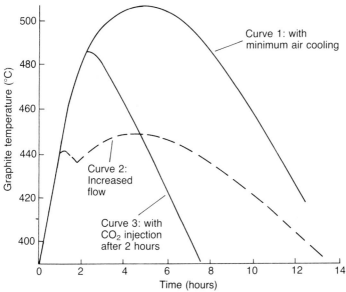

Fig. 3. Graphite temperatures following depressurisation in Magnox reactor

More recent designs of gas-cooled reactors

The above description relates to the early Magnox reactors. The pressure vessels of the later Magnox reactors are in concrete rather than steel, and the whole circuit is much more integrated. Depressurisation faults are less serious on such reactors. The AGR also has a concrete pressure vessel, and its enriched uranium fuel is in the ceramic temperature-resistant form of uranium oxide, while the fuel can is made of stainless steel, which is more robust than Magnox. These design changes allow higher powers to be achieved without reducing safety margins.

Safety procedures and infrastructures

The Russian type of RBMK reactor is one which we have chosen not to build in the UK; though doubtless we could have operated it safely, by giving it great care and attention. But the RBMK's fundamental weaknesses of a substantial and rapid-acting positive power coefficient, and the need to place undue reliance on operational procedures, are serious design defects. British gas-cooled reactors just could not fail in the same way. Moreover, even though we do not need to place the same degree of reliance on our operators to ensure safety, in fact we take great care to ensure that they are well trained, that they put safety first, and that they are properly supervised. We lay very great stress on the following priciples.

First of all our operators are professional engineers, with specialist training and a proper understanding of reactor engineering. We regard it as essential that they should really understand the machine they are responsible for. Secondly, any planned departures from normal operations are very carefully analysed and, if authorised, are strictly controlled. I seriously doubt whether we would ever be allowed to do the kind of experiment that was being undertaken at Chernobyl. The details of the Chernobyl experiment do not seem to have been written down properly; and, worse still, even what was written down was not adhered to. Procedures in force in the UK just would not permit that to happen. This extreme care is part of what we refer to as the safety infrastructure.

Our power station managers basically have two objectives. One is, of course, to produce economic electricity. The other, which is overriding, is to produce that electricity safely. They know that they are just as responsible for safety as they are for effective production. Within the Central Electricity Generating Board we have our own safety organisation, for which I am responsible, which looks at the safety analysis. If a man wants to make any change at all to a reactor he first has to describe in detail what he is going to do, and why it can be regarded as safe. This is looked at by my organisation; and we also bring in independent experts who form a safety committee that looks at the proposal. In addition, there is the government's Nuclear Inspectorate that makes sure that my group is doing its job properly. So we have defence in depth, and a philosophy that makes safety paramount.

The Russians not only had a bad design of reactor, but they also had people who were trying to cut corners—people who were doing an experiment whose details had not been properly analysed. Moreover, there were six breaches of the Russians' own operating rules. In the UK such operating rules have the force of the law. But, in addition, if our operators were inadvertently to breach an operating rule, then very rapidly the reactor would be shut down; or else remedial measures would be taken to make sure that the error was put right. For our Magnox reactors it is not only the safety engineering, which I have briefly outlined, which keeps us safe; the safety infrastructure and our whole approach to safety is probably even more important.

Emergency planning

Finally, a word on emergency planning. In the UK our plans have evolved over the years, and there is a general impresssion that these emergency plans only extend out to 1½ miles. How can this be reconciled with Chernobyl, where people needed to be evacuated out to 18 miles? This is a good question. It comes down to how one plans against highly improbable events.

From all our studies of reactor accidents, it is highly unlikely in the UK that with our reactors we shall have any radioactive release that will require any evacuation at all. The maximum credible accident, with just the right size of break in a pipe, gives a 1 in 100 probability of a fire in a single fuel channel. If that happened, one would still theoretically not need to evacuate anyone, although the dose could go above the minimum action level. The figure of 1½ miles has been determined with that in mind. The police and the local authorities have very precise plans that they would put into action. Specific police are available at all times to set up road blocks, issue iodate tablets, and do anything else necessary within this 1½ mile radius.

Beyond that, in the UK, we have a system of general emergency plans to cover all sorts of eventualities—not just nuclear accidents, but including major chemical explosions and plane crashes. These plans are the responsibility of the county authorities. If a large accident should ever happen, the county authorities would bring their county disaster plans into effect. The system is not as precise as for the 1½ miles zone: the response would be a flexible one. Police would move in to deal with the situation where it arose.

The possibility of a large accident has not been ignored in the UK, contrary to some suggestions in the press. We treat it in a way that I believe is adequate, but which is being reviewed at the present time (September 1986). Attention is focussed first on avoiding accidents, and secondly on dealing with the biggest that are thought credible—while retaining a generally flexible approach to the large, but hardly credible, accidents that could theoretically occur.

The biological effects of radiation

PETER SAUNDERS

Public anxiety about nuclear power is centred on the possibility of harm, in particular cancer and genetic effects, resulting from exposure to radiation.

Damage mechanisms

As radiation interacts with matter it loses some of its energy and produces ionisation—the ejection of an electron from an atom, leaving it positively charged. This ionisation can lead to chemical changes which, in living tissue, can result in biological damage. The critical targets appear to be the DNA molecules, present in every cell of the body, that carry the information required for the development and division of the cell, and for the growth, proper function and reproduction of the organism. The radiation may alter a small part of the molecule, or it may break one or both of the strands of the DNA, in the chromosomes that are visible under a microscope, destroying or altering some of the information carried. Damaged DNA can to a considerable extent be repaired by enzymes in the cell. However, in some cases the DNA survives in an unrepaired state, which can then be transmitted to large numbers of daughter cells by the normal processes of cell replication. Cells that have been changed in such a way are not necessarily dangerous—indeed many such changes occur normally during the lifetime of any organism. However, in some cases the altered cells can multiply in such a way that a cancer results; or, if the damage occurs in a germinal cell that is itself later involved in the reproductive process, effects may be seen in later generations. Another possibility is that the cell is so seriously damaged that it dies. This is significant only if very many cells are killed, since cells are dying and being replaced all the time, and most organs contain far more cells than are needed to maintain normal function.

45

Units

Before discussing the numerical relationships between different doses of radiation and their biological effects, we need to introduce the units that are used to measure radiation. Since it is the transfer of energy from the radiation to the target that causes the damage, the first unit is a measure of that energy transfer: it is the quantity of energy transferred from the radiation to a unit mass of the target material. The unit is the *gray*, after a physicist who studied under Rutherford and devoted much of his life to the medical uses of radiation. It is a unit of *absorbed dose*, and one gray is equal to one joule of energy per kilogram of target matter. Absorbed dose was formerly expressed in a much smaller unit called the rad; 1 gray equals 100 rad.

However, equal absorbed doses do not necessarily have equal biological effects. A given amount of energy in the form of alpha particles, for example, is about 20 times as effective at causing biological damage as the same amount of energy in the form of beta particles, gamma rays or X-rays, because of the much higher ionisation density per unit track length. To take such differences into account we use a unit called the *sievert*, after the Swedish scientist Rolf Sievert. It is a unit of *dose equivalent* which is equal to the absorbed dose (in joules per kilogram) multiplied by a factor that takes into account the different effectiveness in causing damage of the different types of radiation. Dose equivalent was formerly expressed in a unit called the rem, and 1 sievert equals 100 rem. The term dose equivalent is frequently abbreviated to dose. In terms of human susceptibility, the sievert is a very large unit, so the units commonly used are the millisievert (one thousandth of a sievert) and the microsievert (one millionth of a sievert).

A useful measure of radiation dose to a group of people or a whole population is the *collective dose*; this is just the average dose times the number of people receiving that dose. The unit is the *man sievert*.

The natural background and other sources of radiation

The best way to get a feel for the size of these units is to consider the doses received from the natural background and from common sources such as medical X-rays (Fig. 1). The average dose in Britain from natural background radiation is about 2 millisieverts

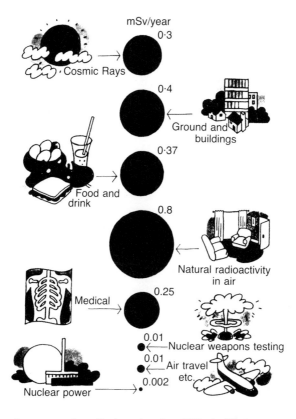

Fig. 1. Sources of radiation in the UK (millisieverts a year) (National Radiological Protection Board)

(one five-hundredth of a sievert) a year. This radiation comes from outer space (cosmic radiation); from rocks, soil and building materials (terrestrial gamma radiation); from the air we breathe, which contains the naturally radioactive daughter products of the gases radon and thoron that are emitted from the ground (radon decay products); and from the naturally radioactive materials such as radionuclides from the uranium and thorium decay series and potassium-40 that are present in what we eat and drink, and irradiate the body tissues internally (internal radiation).

Natural background radiation differs considerably in different parts of the world. Many parts of Britain have levels over twice the average, and in some houses in which there are particularly high radon concentrations individuals may get as much as 100 milli-sieverts a year, 50 times the average.

Other typical figures are 20 microsieverts from a chest X-ray, 10 microsieverts a year from the debris from the atmospheric testing of nuclear weapons during the 1950s and 1960s, 4 microsieverts a year (in Britain) from the natural radioactivity dispersed into the environment with the fly ash that is released during the burning of coal, and 1.5 microsieverts a year (average in Britain) from discharges from the nuclear power industry. A representative figure for the annual dose received from the nuclear power industry by the most highly exposed individuals in Britain is 1 millisievert, or about half the average natural background dose. The average annual exposure of radiation workers in Britain is about 1.4 millisieverts.

Risk estimates
The three kinds of effect of radiation to be considered are cell killing, cancer and genetic (Fig. 2 and Table 1).

Table 1. Risk estimates

Cell killing

   ~ 10 gray fatal
   Below 1 gray no early effects

Radiation-induced cancer

   ~ 1 in 100 per sievert

Genetic effects

   ~ 1 in 125 per sievert (all generations)
   ~ 1 in 250 per sievert (first and second generations)

Effects at low doses

   Linear hypothesis: risk proportional to dose
   Probably overestimates risk for beta and gamma radiation

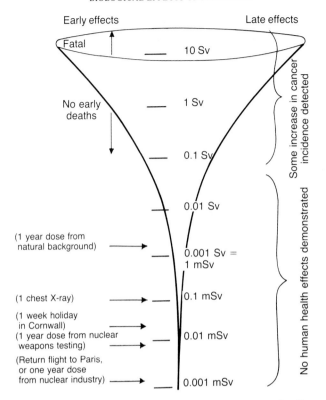

Fig. 2. Effects of radiation (United Nations Scientific Committee on the Effects of Atomic Radiation)

Cell killing

Cell killing is only important if sufficiently large doses of radiation are received in a sufficiently brief period. An absorbed dose of 10 gray or more delivered to the whole or a substantial part of the body within a few minutes is almost invariably fatal. A single absorbed dose of about 4 gray will result in a one in two chance of death in the absence of medical treatment. The same dose delivered gradually over a year, however, would probably be tolerated because of the action of the body's natural repair processes. The ability of radiation to kill cells is, of course, the basis of radiotherapy, where localised doses of tens of grays are used to treat cancers and other growths. Cell killing effects are

49

characterised by a threshold below which no significant effects occur; there are in general no observable effects below about 1 gray.

Radiation-induced cancer

Unlike the cell killing effects, which in general appear within a relatively short time after exposure and exhibit a threshold, cancer and genetic effects are delayed; and it must be assumed that there is no threshold below which one can be certain that no harm will result. However, there is no evidence of effects at low doses (below a few tens of millisieverts), and the universal and inescapable natural radiation background and the 'natural' prevalence of cancer and genetic defects are such that it will probably never be possible to prove the existence or absence of a threshold.

There is a vast amount of data on the effects of radiation on cells and animals, and there are a rather limited number of cases where a small excess cancer incidence has been found in groups of people exposed to sufficiently high doses of radiation, mostly above 1 sievert. However, the chain of events leading from radiation-induced damage in a cell to a developed cancer is far from well understood. Even when a link has been established between a radiation exposure and a subsequent cancer, the radiation exposure itself may be only a necessary factor and not a sufficient cause of the cancer. Subsequent radiation exposures, exposures to chemicals, or metabolic changes may be required before a tumour results. Such processes take many years: latent periods are typically 5–10 years for leukaemias and 15–30 years for solid cancers.

While most but not all cancers can be induced by radiation, it is not possible to distinguish between a radiation-induced cancer and any other cancer. The only way in which the number of cancers that may be caused by an exposure to radiation can be predicted is on the basis of epidemiological studies of groups that have been exposed to radiation in the past. These are the survivors of the Hiroshima and Nagasaki bombs, patients who have received large doses of radiation for therapeutic or diagnostic purposes, and—in the days before radiation effects were well understood— workers who had been exposed to high levels of radiation, such as radiographers, watch-dial painters using radium, and miners of uranium and other hard rocks. The distribution of doses and the number of people exposed as a result of the Chernobyl accident are not yet known in sufficient detail to enable any reliable estimates to be made of the possible long term consequences. Preliminary indications, however, suggest that a sufficient number of people may have received high enough doses to result in a detectable increase in cancer incidence. It will clearly be of great importance to monitor the health of these people carefully over a long period.

The evidence has been exhaustively reviewed and assessed by national and international scientific bodies such as the International Commission on Radiological Protection, the United Nations Committee on the Effects of Atomic Radiation, and the Biological Effects of Ionising Radiation Committee of the US National Academy of Science. The consensus view of these bodies is that there is about a one in 100 risk of fatal cancer developing for each sievert of radiation dose received, over and above the doses received from the natural background, with an uncertainty in this risk of a factor of two; for safety purposes this uncertainty is of no significance.

Genetic effects

The basic process that can ultimately lead to a cancer or genetic defect is damage to a DNA molecule. As with cancer, however, the mechanism by which a mutation in a cell leads to a genetic defect is complex and not fully understood. If the mutated cell dies, or is not actually involved in the fertilisation process, there will be no genetic effect. Also, if the new individual created at conception is not viable and dies at an early stage of embryonic development, it will probably not be detected. Most species seem to have evolved a protective mechanism by which faulty embryos are rejected; chromosome alterations are frequently found in spontaneous abortions. Genetic effects of radiation, ranging from trivial to lethal, have been observed in studies of animal populations. No unequivocal evidence of similar effects in humans has yet appeared at any dose level. Even in the Hiroshima and Nagasaki studies, no genetic defects that can be ascribed to the radiation from the bombs have been observed in any of the children subsequently conceived by the exposed parents. All estimates of possible genetic effects in humans, therefore, have to be based on extrapolation from results obtained with other

51

species, notably mice. Such extrapolation involves considerable uncertainties.

The ICRP, UNSCEAR and BEIR analyses suggest that for humans there would be about a one in 50 risk of a genetic defect occurring for each sievert of radiation dose received, over and above the doses received from the natural background. This risk would be spread over all subsequent generations. These estimates refer to the risk of a genetic defect occurring following exposure of a hypothetical population of fertile individuals irradiated prior to conception of their offspring. In practice, some of the dose to which a real population is exposed will have no genetic significance because it will be received when no more children are likely to be conceived. Taking this factor into account reduces the risk, expressed in terms of a given total lifetime radiation dose to a given real population, to one in 125 per sievert.

In summary, a dose of 1 sievert is associated with a 1 in 100 risk of fatal cancer in the exposed individual and a somewhat lower risk of a serious genetic defect appearing, spread over all subsequent generations. These figures are unlikely to be in error by more than a factor of two.

Extrapolation to low doses

Most of the evidence of radiation-induced cancer relates to doses of one sievert or more. There are a few cases where excess cancers have been found following doses of about one tenth of a sievert, but there are not enough data to provide quantitative risk estimates. There is no reliable evidence of any effects associated with the doses received from the natural background, which results in lifetime doses of about 130 millisieverts in the UK.

There are many parts of the world where background radiation levels are higher than the UK average, as a result of local geology or high altitudes. Attempts have been made to find correlations between natural cancer incidence and background radiation levels in such areas and no statistically significant effects have been found.

There have also been detailed studies of cancer incidence among workers in the nuclear industry, where typical radiation exposures are 1.4 millisieverts a year, or less than one tenth of a sievert in a working life, which is less than the natural background dose. No consistent pattern emerges from these studies, an indication that any effect from radiation is too small to be detectable.

These negative results confirm that the risk estimates derived from observations following doses of 1 sievert or more, are unlikely to underestimate seriously the risks at much lower levels. The question remains, what is the true risk at low levels? Does a dose of a few millisieverts—a typical annual occupational dose—result in a risk of one thousandth of that at a few sieverts, typical of the doses at which cancers have actually been observed? And does a dose of a few microsieverts, the average dose received by members of the UK public from the activities of the UK nuclear industry, result in any risk at all? Such questions may never be answered by observation, because of the size of the population that would have to be studied to give statistically significant results. They can only be answered indirectly through an understanding of the basic processes involved in radiation damage and its repair. The simplest assumption to make is that harm is directly proportional to dose, with no threshold. This is known as the linear hypothesis, and is widely accepted as the correct basis for radiological protection purposes.

On the basis of this hypothesis, in the UK about 1000 cancer deaths per year and about 300 genetic defects per year might be ascribed to natural background radiation, although there is no evidence that such effects occur. It is worth noting that cancer kills about 140 000 people in the UK each year. On the same hypothesis, just over one cancer death per year and, if the exposure continued for enough generations for an equilibrium to be established, about one genetic defect a year might be ascribed to the exposure of the population to the activities of the UK nuclear industry. The existence of repair processes within the body probably means that the true risks are even lower, and at such low levels of exposure a zero risk is not incompatible with the evidence.

Chernobyl

The average radiation exposure within 30 kilometres of Chernobyl was of the order of a thirtieth of a sievert. That is well below the dose level at which there is evidence of enhanced cancer rates.

It is important to remember, when one reads about the possible number of deaths that have resulted from accidents like the Windscale fire in 1957, Three Mile Island, and now Chernobyl, that those deaths are almost always calculated on the assumption that the linear hypothesis is correct. For example, the prediction that the release from the Windscale fire in 1957 might eventually result in about 30 deaths in the UK, is based on the linear hypothesis. Although a large number of people received doses, the actual doses were so low that it is quite possible that the true figure is going to be much less. That will certainly apply to TMI, where the individual doses were very low indeed. It remains to be seen if the same applies to Chernobyl, when we are able to draw conclusions from the many detailed studies that will have to be carried out among the population that were exposed within that 30 kilometre region.

Radiation protection policy

JOHN DUNSTER

The fundamental policy underlying occupational radiation protection starts with a basic system of dose limitation, which is recommended by the International Commission on Radiological Protection. There are three principal components. First of all one should not do something involving radiation unless some net benefit is obtained; this is a fairly elementary principle but is not always observed. The second component has been called 'optimisation of protection', which means that work should be organised so that doses are as low as reasonably achievable. The basic reason is that we have to assume for protection purposes that there may still be some risk even at small doses. So a simple limit is never good enough: even being below the limit leaves one with a residual risk, and if one can easily do better then one should do so. This basic and most important principle is that doses should be kept as low as they reasonably can—reasonable being a difficult word to interpret legally, but not impossible. Finally, some limits on dose are needed, because one wants to make sure that no individual is put at excessive risk. If total population doses are kept as low as reasonably achievable, one may find that the most reasonably achievable way is to load all the dose on one man, which would be unfair; so individual dose limits are also necessary. Furthermore, the whole concept of optimisation is not a certain one: there is a lot of judgement involved. If one's judgement is seriously wrong one could be in trouble; but the dose limits provide a safety net to prevent one from being seriously wrong.

Radiation doses are usually given in millisieverts. The background is about 2 millisieverts per year; the maximum for a worker is 50 millisieverts per year; the maximum per single year for a member of the public is 5 millisieverts; and there is an overriding requirement for the public that in the long term the dose should not exceed 1 millisievert per year on average. So we are controlling the public doses down to about natural background, and somewhat higher for radiation workers.

The choice of these limits is not simple. In the first place some estimate of the cancer risk must be made: a figure of 1 in 100 per sievert is mentioned in Peter Saunders' paper. ICRP takes that as a general working rule. The risks may be slightly higher, or may be slightly lower at low doses and low dose rates; but that is a good working figure. There is a similar risk of serious hereditary defect. But this tells us nothing about the choice of a limit; it merely tells us how dangerous radiation is.

The next stage we have to go through is to choose some limit of risk which we are prepared to regard as acceptable; and more particularly, that we are prepared to regard as the starting point of the *un*acceptable. Exceeding the dose limit, which means making someone exceed the preselected limit of risk, is a criminal offence in the UK. So this is not in any sense a target: it is a figure above which one really feels one is in trouble. The figure adopted by the ICRP is determined by comparison with fatal risks in industry generally worldwide. They take, broadly speaking, a figure which at the average dose gives a single year's risk of a little less than 1 chance in 10 000 of being killed by one's occupation. That is not trivial, but it is not particularly high: there are very few years of life when the risk of dying in a year is less than one chance in 1000. So one chance in 10 000 is quite a small risk; but it is one that is regarded as significant, and basically one that would be unaccept-able in general industrial situations, though it has to be accepted in some. The limit applies to the total dose to the individual from all artificial sources of radiation. So it cannot be used as the dose limit for any particular operation. One has to make quite sure that the total of *all* the sources to which an individual is exposed is within the dose limit.

Accidents

So much for the routine situation. Interest in this seminar is focused on Chernobyl and on accidents. It is not sensible to apply a limit to an accident. Accidents do not take account of limits, and they may do things that one had no intention of accepting. So a limit is not a relevant feature. What one needs is some sort of action *level* to indicate, when there has been an accident, whether or not something should be done. The term used in the UK is 'emergency reference level'. First, there is a low level, which is really a *non*-action level: it is a level below which one really does not believe that any action is justified. Then, at a higher level of dose, comes a point where one thinks that, whatever happens, one should try to take action, however difficult. Those two numbers differ, depending on whose advice you use, by a factor of about 5 or 10. The important feature is that they leave one with an area of judgement in between: the main thing one needs to retain in an accident is a sense of judgement.

The initial problems which one is faced with in an accidental release of radioactivity to the environment can be summed up fairly quickly. Somebody is going to be exposed to a cloud of radioactive gas. They may inhale it. They may get direct radiation from beta or gamma rays in the cloud. As the cloud gets deposited on the ground, they will get radiation from the ground. All these happen fairly quickly. In the case of the people who were on site at Chernobyl, the gamma dose from the cloud was what was responsible for most of the deaths; but the beta dose from the cloud and from contamination of clothing and skin gave severe skin burns, and was a significant factor in some cases.

Soon afterwards, the deposit of activity on the ground starts getting into the environment and moving through the environmental pathways. It may go through grass to cows, and so into milk. It will get into meat and vegetables. It will deposit on surface vegetables, without having to go through the soil. So there is quite a complicated situation. With materials of significant half-life, like caesium-137 (which has a half-life of about 30 years), the whole of the environmental network will be involved. All this must be taken into account when one is deciding on the countermeasures to be taken against the longer-term problems.

The countermeasures available when an accident occurs are fairly limited: staying in the house, keeping doors and windows closed, and so on. That was done in the area around Chernobyl. It gives a significant protection factor, perhaps amounting to 5 or 10 if the house is fairly well closed. If they are available, drugs like potassium iodide or potassium iodate can be issued. If they are issued early enough they are useful as a protection, because they block the transfer of iodine to the thyroid; but they do nothing against direct radiation, and nothing for materials other than iodine. However, since iodine is a major product of most reactor accidents, the precaution is worthwhile.

When one has had time to think, and not before, one considers evacuation. Generally speaking it is not desirable to evacuate in the middle of an accident, unless one thinks the accident is going on for rather a long time and is getting worse, because the chances are that one will take people out of shelter into a more hazardous situation. Once one has somewhere to put people, and knows that they are not being exposed to more danger, evacuation can be useful. The first evacuation at Chernobyl was decided on 34 hours into the accident. It started at 36 hours and was completed 2½ hours later; 45 000 people moved in those 2 hours. The big evacuation, out to the 30 kilometre radius, was not arranged until 8 or 9 days after the event; so there was apparently not a highly organised plan on that scale.

On a longer-term basis one needs to control foodstuffs, particularly milk if the accident is in a milk-producing area. One may have to control water supplies, though that is fairly unimportant in relation to control of foodstuffs. It worried the Russians a great deal, but the actual numbers did not seem to support their worry. Later on still, there may be houses which are not fit to live in or return to; and one may have to consider relocation. One has to apply food bans, and control foodstuffs perhaps for some years—certainly for many months after the event, and perhaps for longer. So the long term effects get quite complicated; and, if they occur over any large area they become dramatically expensive, or possibly dramatically dangerous if the alternative is not having food: given a stark choice between starvation and radiation, the radiation becomes the lesser of the two evils fairly quickly.

The real problem here is to define a basis for a level for action. We start off by having an emergency reference level of dose. That is, we decide on the level of dose at which to take action. For evacuation, in the UK we take action if the whole body dose to the members of public is expected to go above 0.1 gray. The permissible dose to a worker in a year is 0.05 gray; so what we are saying is that if a member of the public is likely to get 2 years' worth of a *worker*'s permissible dose, then evacuation should be seriously considered. If the dose is going to be less, then there is no need for evacuation. Doing something simple like sheltering would be sensible. If something like 0.5 gray is reached, then one should evacuate with a fair degree of certainty. So there is a relation between the magnitude of the emergency reference level, and the level of action that should be taken if it is exceeded.

If one moves on to the control of food, there are real difficulties. The relation between the radioactive concentration in the food which is measured on the day—which is the basis for any decision—and the dose that somebody gets, depends very substantially on the way the radioactive material moves through the environment; how the foodstuffs are shipped and marketed; how people eat them; the quantities they eat; where they get their food from—locally or imported from clean areas—and so on. So deciding on what we call 'derived emergency reference levels', for something measurable like activity in the food, is an exceedingly complicated business.

There was a substantial degree of confusion in Europe following the accident at Chernobyl, just because that degree of complexity was not adequately recognised. Many of the decisions were made without the practical implications being worked through. My guess is that the total cost of the various interventions made in food supplies over the whole of Europe over a 3 month period must run into hundreds of millions of pounds. If, as I believe, those decisions were made on an inadequate technical basis, a lot of that was money wasted.

Effect of Chernobyl on the UK

In general terms, the release from Chernobyl was about 2×10^{18} becquerels. There is some uncertainty about this number because it is easy to determine with a burning reactor; and also because the date at which the radioactivity is defined is important. Iodine has a half-life of eight days, and the release lasted ten; so whether iodine is counted at the beginning or the end introduces a factor of two. The figure of 2×10^{18} becquerels is normalised to the end of the release. Normalised to the same date, iodine-131 gave 2.5×10^{17} becquerels. For comparison, the Windscale accident in 1957, which we thought was quite a serious event, produced 7×10^{14} becquerels—about 350 times less—so the Russians really did have a problem on their hands. There was about 4×10^{16} becquerels of the long-lived caesium-137 (30 year half-life).

We have now done our second, though still fairly crude,

estimate of the consequences for the UK. We have done it for different areas, because we had a situation where the cloud came to the south of England, moved north to Scotland, swung out over the Atlantic, and in a very dilute form came back round the far side of Ireland. Basically it was a single pass, but for some of the time while the cloud was overhead it rained heavily in some places: rain brings the radioactivity out of the cloud and deposits it. We have modelled the effects as accurately as possible. We get for the effective whole body dose in dry areas about 0.03 millisievert. In the wet areas it is about 0.3 millisievert, giving a mean of about 0.05 millisievert. The background every year is about 2 millisievert, so clearly the total dose to the population in the UK is not a serious worry. Thyroid doses were rather higher, though we did not issue stable iodine because all the doses were too low to make that worth while; the mean thyroid dose across the country was about 0.2 millisievert. So none of it is very serious; in fact the whole position in Europe is not serious, with the exception of a few highly localised problems, of which undoubtedly the worst concerns the reindeer in Lapland in the north of Scandinavia. Reindeer eat lichen on the ground and on rocks, and they cover large areas to get nourishment. So they sweep up radioactivity in very large quantities. This has always been known as a problem with fall-out from weapons tests; it is certainly a problem for the Lapps.

Relative levels of risk

Just a final word about the relative levels of risk to which we are all exposed anyway, to provide some sort of comparison. The figure that ICRP uses as an absolute limit for workers is equivalent to about 500 deaths per million man years. But that is the level above which it becomes a criminal offence; and the actual levels that are received as a result of combinations of circumstances correspond to less than 50 deaths per million man years. In comparison (Table 1), normal work is moderately dangerous; having fun—skiing or rock-climbing—can be quite disastrously dangerous. One can also get some pretty high risks just by living. These are substantially increased if one is male, because of motorcycles. There is an observable peak in the accidental death rate in males in their late teens and early twenties in the UK. By the time one is middle-aged the numbers do not bear looking at too closely. Old people at home provide a substantial component of the total accident frequency. So it is not all that easy to make comparisons. All I really want to emphasise is that there are other things besides radiation which should provide cause for thought.

Table 1. *Some levels of fatal risk in England and Wales*

Surgical anaesthesia (1970–73)	40 per million cases
Child-bearing (1974–76)	100 per million births
Natural causes (males 1981)	
Age 15–24	250 per million man years
Age 45–54	5 600 per million man years
Age 65–74	45 000 per million man years
Road accidents (all ages)	120 per million man years
Other accidents (all ages)	67 per million man years
Work (1976–80)	
Vehicle manufacture	13 per million man years
Chemicals	49 per million man years
Quarries	300 per million man years
Fun	
Skiing (France 1974–76)	1.3 per million man *hours*
Rock-climbing (1961)	40 per million man *hours*

Sources: Royal Society; Registrar General; Health and Safety Executive.

Reactor safety philosophy

PIERRE TANGUY

Table 1 lists the five topics I will deal with in this part of the presentation.

Design for safe normal operation and anticipated transients

Design for safe normal operation starts with the identification of risk. Risk is of course related to the existence of fission products. If we want to limit risk, we have to be sure that the fission products will be contained, in any anticipated situation. Figure 1 shows a pressurised water reactor (PWR), corresponding to the Three Mile Island design. The Westinghouse PWR, similar to the one we are building in France, is somewhat different; but the differences hardly alter the safety principles. The fuel is uranium dioxide; the can zircaloy—very similar to the Chernobyl fuel; the coolant pressurised water. In Fig. 1 there are two circuits, or loops—though in French reactors we have either three or four loops. The coolant, after extraction from the core, goes to the steam generator before returning to the inlet to the core.

For the same power in a Magnox reactor there is more mechanical equipment, compared with a PWR. That was one of the reasons why Electricité de France changed from Magnox to PWRs—mainly a question of cost. What is true, and what is very important in relation to the analysis of TMI and Chernobyl, is that the operation of a Magnox reactor is much simpler.

In a Magnox reactor, and in a fast breeder, there is nearly complete separation between the primary circuit, extracting the fission power from the core, and the secondary circuit, taking the power to the turbine. In a PWR—and even more so in a BWR—there is a complex interaction between the behaviour of the secondary circuit and the behaviour of the primary circuit. In a PWR, for instance, there are cases where the operator would not

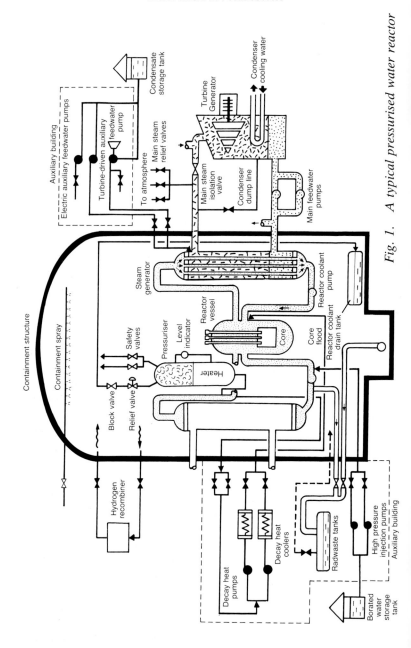

Fig. 1.   A typical pressurised water reactor

Table 1.   The safety of pressurised water reactors

- Design for safe normal operation and anticipated transients

- Defence in depth—design basis accidents

- Actions after Three Mile Island

- Operational experience feedback

- Safety approach reviewed in the light of Chernobyl

know immediately if he has a fault in the primary circuit or in the secondary circuit, because the first signals coming to him would be exactly the same. He would need more analysis to identify firmly what was happening.

In our safety analysis (Table 2) the first two barriers to fission product escape are the fuel can (zirconium alloy), and the pressure vessel and primary circuit envelope. These barriers are necessary to protect the operators from the radioactive products, and to contain the coolant under pressure. If we look only at normal operation and anticipated transients, there is no need for the third barrier, which is a containment structure. Its necessity depends on accident analysis.

To have any safety problems with the first of our barriers, the fuel can, there must be an imbalance between heat production and heat extraction. So we look successively at the various reasons why such an imbalance could occur. I will not go into much detail, but let us first look at excessive power. This was presented by Dr Wright in the context of a reactivity accident, because an increase of reactivity leads to an excess of power.

In a PWR one has the first important aspect, which is its inherent stability due to the negative coefficient of reactivity: reactivity falls as power increases. The power coefficient was very important in the Chernobyl accident, given the reactor situation at the time of the accident. With the RBMK reactor the coefficient was positive; a negative coefficient like that in the PWR is far more desirable. There are great safety advantages in having that first level of inherent stability, whereby if there is an increase of power, there is a limited reaction which tends to oppose the increase. In contrast, if the coefficient is positive, when the power is increased

Table 2.   Design for safe normal operation and anticipated transients

- Identification of risks; the theory of barriers

- Fuel behaviour; imbalance between heat production and extraction

- Excessive power

  Stability due to negative reactivity coefficient
  Insertion of control rods: controlled on coolant temperature
  Scram: on flux and gradient
  Boration: on low coolant temperature

- Insufficient cooling

  Compensation of water leakage
  Scram: on fuel temperature, pressure, pump failure
  Scram: on steam generator low level

- Decay heat removal

  Natural convection
  Emergency feed water
  Heat removal system

- Vessel and primary circuit

  Choice of materials; design codes
  Water quality control
  In-service inspection

- Auxiliary systems

- Quality assurance

there is a positive feedback—a kind of chain progression. Then of course, as a further safety factor we have the system of control rods, regulated by signals from the coolant temperature. We can also use the neutron flux or flux gradient, using the differential coefficient with time to trigger a scram (i.e. shutdown) system. And finally in the PWR there is also a system for introducing boron in the form of boric acid into the water.

In other respects there may be no inherent stability, even with a PWR. When we start losing water there is no inherent means of feeding more water into the system, so we have to rely on safety engineering features and finally on safety systems. It is the same for decay heat removal: we can never completely shut down a reactor, and must be able to extract the after-heat coming from the fission products. Here we are helped by natural convection, but that is not enough: we also need a heat sink. There are some reactor types which in this regard also have an inherent degree of stability: that is, when we increase the temperature of the system, we increase the rate of extraction of heat, so that we finally reach a stable level. This can be the case, for instance, for fast breeders of a limited size (e.g. in the case of the 200 megawatt Phénix fast breeder). It is no longer the case when the size is increased to 1200 megawatts, because external heat rejection is then insufficient.

Other safety issues concern the primary and the secondary circuits, and engineering quality assurance (Table 3). What is really essential is being sure that the reactor has been designed and built as it should have been, and that there have been no big errors in manufacture. The quality is dependent on the professionalism of the company which carries out the engineering study, manufactures the components and builds the plant. Certainly no regulatory requirements, not even some external surveillance, can provide quality assurance. Having checked that the proper quality has been obtained, action can be taken to correct any deficiencies; but in the last resort it is only the man in the workshop who can give the necessary degree of assurance.

Failures in quality lead to immediate costs in availability. Figure 2 gives the availability factor for the 900 megawatt PWR units we

Table 3.   Quality assurance

- Quality for studies, manufacture and erection assured by professionalism and by control by company

- Electricité de France responsible for surveillance and quality assurance programme

- Safety authorities exert surveillance and audits at given steps

- Analysis of tests and operational experience should allow detection of deficiencies

---

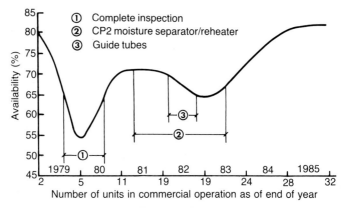

Fig. 2.   Availability trend for French 900 megawatt PWR units

have in Electricité de France. There were 32 in operation at the end of 1985. The early decrease was a consequence of a regulatory requirement, that we should shut down a plant after 18 months of operation to have a complete inspection of the pressure vessel and primary circuit. We had a big reduction in availability due to quality deficiencies, one on the secondary side and one on the primary side (the rupture inside the core of the pins of the control rod guide tubes). In contrast, the Chernobyl reactor was the 'best' Soviet operating unit. But when a reactor is apparently operating well it may be necessary to consider whether the operator should be more careful.

Defence in depth—design basis accidents
I come now to the safety analysis. We design for normal operation, including normal transients. Then we look at what could go wrong. There is a general method which is coming from the USA that is widely used. It is a classification of the events which have to be taken into account in design, in four categories. For each of them the analysis of the event must show that the radiological consequences are limited. In categories 1 and 2—events with a probability that is greater than 1 in 100 per year—the radioactive release outside must be within the authorised limits. Category 4 are hypothetical events with probabilities between 1 in 10 000 and 1 in 1000 000 per year, which is a very low figure; even their

68

evaluation has serious technical difficulties. For these hypothetical events, if the evaluation is right, the radiological consequence is limited at the site boundary to about 0.15 sievert equivalent.

We have to provide safety systems incorporating redundancy; that is, any time we need one safety system to protect the plant, we must provide at least two safety systems, because the regulation requires that we assume the single-failure criterion—the first safety system might not operate on demand. What looks really strange in the Chernobyl accident—it is quite precise in the Soviet rules—is that there did not seem to be any redundancy on one of their shutdown systems.

Redundancy is not enough: we also need diversity. We have to be on our guard against the possibility of a common mode failure; that is a single fault which—because the design or operation is defective—could put out of service *two* systems, causing a loss of redundancy. In the past we have also introduced for most of the systems a degree of physical separation, initially as a protection against fire—which is a permanent concern of safety on all plants. It is also useful as a defence against sabotage.

Next, the containment. For normal operation and anticipated transients, containment is unnecessary: it can be demonstrated that without containment the radioactivity release would be acceptable. In fact containment was not introduced in the early days of nuclear energy: in the 1950s, when PWRs were developed in the USA, the idea was to build them without containment. But then, during the first real accident studies, it was realised that for a large failure in the primary circuit envelope—even if a failure of the pressure vessel itself is not considered possible—there would be a cooling transient which would be so serious as to cause quite a significant failure of the first barrier—the fuel cans. The two barriers between the fission products and the environment would then be breached, and large amounts of radioactivity would escape. The calculations at that time demonstrated that one could have a plant without containment, but one should then have an uninhabited exclusion zone, out to a radius (for a 1000 megawatt reactor) of 30 kilometres. When one remembers that the Chernobyl reactor is a 1000 megawatt unit, that the accident was not contained, and that they had to evacuate a 30 kilometre radius region, it seems that the people in the 1950s had a fairly realistic view of the situation.

So containment was introduced, for what was called the maximum credible accident. This term is used in Dr Wright's paper, but in France we no longer use it. It corresponds to the largest break in the primary circuit thought possible at that time, which would give a pressure inside the containment of the order of five or six atmospheres.

The general safety level of the plant can be judged from a probabilistic risk assessment.

Actions after Three Mile Island

After TMI there was an evolution in safety thinking (Table 4). In TMI the initial event was very trivial. There was of course a human error—there is always a human error. Many automatic systems went into operation; and in the accident all the automatic systems worked almost perfectly. There was another minor error somewhere in the valves, but it was not very significant. The reactor was shut down automatically by the shutdown system and this also worked well. So everything was operating properly. The reactor was shut down and was going to be cooled. Then there was one failure of equipment. A valve that had opened automatically during the transient did not close. That was really the only mechanical equipment failure which was independent of the

Table 4. Actions after Three Mile Island

- TMI lessons learnt
- Human factor
    Man–machine interface
    Operator training for accidents
- Loss of redundant systems
    Station black-out
    Anticipated transient without scram; loss of feed water, of heat sink
- Role of containment as ultimate barrier
- Off-site emergency planning

operators. After that there was a 'human factor event'. If the operators had realised what was happening in the reactor, if they had closed the second valve, they could have immediately stopped the sequence and nobody would have heard the name of TMI. They did not think of doing that for several hours, and when they did so it was too late.

There was an automatic safety system, which is very important in PWRs—a safety injection system which is redundant, diverse etc. When the situation became difficult at TMI this safety system went automatically into operation; but the men also went into operation and shut it down. So the TMI accident was really a human factor accident; and that is why the first lesson of TMI was the importance of the human factor. Nobody was saying that the design was not good, but obviously it did not foresee the possibility of inappropriate human action. When we heard from the Russians that this was also the main lesson from Chernobyl, we were not so surprised. The lesson relates to the man–machine interface—that is, the need to give an operator the proper information relevant to safety, and at the proper time. There is also the issue of operator training for the prevention of accidents, and all the questions of procedures that were mentioned by Dr Wright.

After TMI, much more work was done on the human factor. There were also improvements in the safety design, because it was not after all the worst imaginable accident—all the systems had worked well, and no external system was lost. But we needed to ask ourselves what would happen if we lost, for instance, the whole electricity supply, both external and internal; or if a scram system which was redundant but not diverse was not operating; or if we lost all the feed water to the secondary side, or if we lost our heat sink. After TMI we looked at all these things in France.

The human factor

These PWRs are very complex in their operation. It is difficult in an awkward situation for the operator to be sure of what is happening. Obviously, during the TMI accident sequence, the operators had no idea of what was really happening in the core. For that type of situation Electricité de France has introduced special procedures, called 'ultimate procedures'. We do not ask the operator to try to understand what has happened in his reactor; we just want him to look at a few very simple things. Is at least one steam generator available? Or is there no steam generator available? Is safety injection in service or not? Then a glance at a few parameters. What is the temperature of the coolant compared with the saturation temperature?—to see if the water is going to boil. What is the temperature and rate of increase of temperature with time? With a few such parameters, and looking at the status of the steam generators and safety injection, we can give the operator precise instructions with the objective of saving the core.

To put this type of procedure to work in the plant, Electricité de France has introduced a degree of *human* redundancy. For normal operation, or even in case of accident, the only people responsible for the operation of the plant are the operators. If there is an event, there are automatic actions and diagnosis. But for the past five years we have also introduced in the control room a safety engineer on shift. He has an engineering degree, and is specially trained in safety matters. He does not take part in normal operation, but is called upon any time that something unusual happens. If there is any unusual event he is called and goes to the control room. He follows the behaviour of the reactor with a special panel. If at any time he realises that the parameters are not following the right lines, that something is going wrong, he asks the operator to use the special ultimate procedure in case of emergency; then he is also responsible for accident supervision.

We have tested this type of procedure using simulators, and it looks effective. It turns out that human relations, which at first seemed likely to create problems between the engineer and the operators, do not raise any difficulties. So although this is a burden for the company—we have had to recruit 160 engineers, who stay in that position only for about three years—we think it is a good investment. In fact, when they are later used elsewhere, they are considered very good material for the operation of nuclear plants.

Safety design

I should like to give an example of what we did in Electricité de France after TMI to face the problem of the possible complete loss of all electricity supplies. On the main line we have now added a small turbine, and coupled to it a generator. Due to the residual heat, steam is produced from the outlet of the steam generator. With this small generator we can produce electricity, so that we have electricity available for the various safety systems; but, more important, we can power a special pump and send water into the primary coolant plant, just at the primary coolant pump seals; the risk was that loss of electricity would induce damage to the seals and so affect the primary circuit. This is a solution which we have adopted in all units. A further step is to have one gas turbine on each site, which can feed electricity to any of the units—we have up to six on our sites.

In TMI there was a very large radioactivity release from the fuel, and quite a significant radioactivity release from the primary circuit. But there was no significant release into the environment, because the containment building played a very useful role as an ultimate barrier for radioactive containment. It was not designed for that purpose exactly: it was designed to cope with a maximum credible accident, and what happened at TMI was certainly an accident beyond that. Fortunately the safety margin in the design of the TMI building was such that it was able to contain the radioactivity very efficiently. But it was not clear that this would always be the case for an accident sequence slightly different from that at TMI. So in order to draw all the lessons from TMI, we have looked at all possible sequences where the integrity of the last barrier would be challenged. That is why we have introduced one further safety provision in our French reactors.

On a station with two units of 900 megawatts there is an opening, in each of the containment buildings, which is used during commissioning or pressure-testing of the building. It is also used ten years later for the required periodic pressure-testing of the containment, and then it is closed. We decided that we could use that opening for a very specific system, to be used only in extreme urgency. By introducing special manual valves (because we do not want this opening to be opened in error) we can depressurise the atmosphere within the building through a coarse filtering system, made of sand. The efficiency would of course be zero for the noble gases krypton and xenon; but for filtering aerosols of caesium and iodine it gives an efficiency of 90%—which means that only 10% of these volatile fission products would leave the plant through the filter. This would allow us to depressurise the containment building in the case of a slow build-up of pressure, so that we could be sure that it would retain its integrity, while at the same time limiting the radioactive release to the environment.

Off-site emergency planning

The last lesson learned from TMI was that even if we do our best to prevent any accident, or to ensure that if an accident occurs it has a limited radioactive effect on the environment, we must still be prepared to take appropriate measures in case something serious happens. In particular, we need off-site emergency preparations (Tables 5 and 6). From the evaluation of the radioactive release thought possible for the most serious accidents in our plants, and using the reference levels coming from the International Commission on Radiological Protection, the European Commission and the International Atomic Energy Agency, this gives a maximum radius for the zone which might have to be evacuated of 5 kilometres. The zone where the authorities could ask people to stay at home to take the benefit of the shielding effect of buildings would be of 10 kilometres radius. It is obvious that it would be much more difficult for many sites in France and elsewhere in western Europe, if not impossible, to have a feasible emergency plan if we had to go much further than that.

Summary

The main points of our safety approach are summarised in Table 7. First we must start with a proven design. If it is not already proven,

Table 5.   Dose reference levels for French emergency plans (origin EEC; ICRP; IAEA)

- Evacuation: equivalent whole body dose 50–500 millisieverts (5–50 rem)

- Confinement: 5–50 millisieverts (0.5–5 rem)

Table 6.   Reference distances from EdF plant for emergency plans

- Evacuation: up to 5 kilometres

- Confinement: up to 10 kilometres

- Restrictions on food and water consumption: to be decided by health authorities

Table 7. Safety approach

- Proven design with adequate quality assurance

- Consistency check (probability risk assessment, incident analysis)

- Improvements in handling human factor

- Operator training for accidents

- Containment behaviour in the case of severe accidents

- Emergency preparedness

- Residual risks v. nuclear energy benefits

but is a new concept, such as for instance a fast breeder, we have to be very cautious, taking several steps, and only going to the next step when we have acquired sufficient experience from the previous step. That is why with the fast breeder at Creys-Malville, after reaching full power at the end of September 1986, we will wait for two years before ordering a new unit of this type. In the case of the PWR we took a design which already had many years of experience in the USA; so there are still some reference plants in the USA which are ten years in advance of our own.

Then we need proper quality assurance. This is very important. We need to verify the overall safety of the plant, using both reliability analysis and—what is possibly even more important in practice—analysis of operational experience from other people and from our own plants. We have improved many aspects of operation, taking into account the human factor. We have implemented a special programme to be sure that the possibility of accidents will not be regarded as a theoretical concept for operators. Not only should they realise that severe accidents may happen; but also that they may happen to them. They have to be prepared to take appropriate action. We think we have improved the behaviour of the containment in case of severe accidents. One very important aspect is the possibility of a hydrogen explosion, which could ruin the containment building. We consider it absolutely necessary to have firm evidence that this will not be the case.

After all that, we have to convince the public that, while there is still a residual risk, it is limited in comparison with the very obvious and significant benefits resulting from the use of nuclear power.

Discussion

Price

Could I begin the questions by putting one to John Dunster.

There is a general feeling in Europe, which you echoed, that the regulations which the various countries imposed over food controls were fairly abitrary. Is there any chance of securing international agreement at a sensible level? What is happening about that?

Dunster

Reaching agreement will be difficult, but something is being done about it, in the hope that it might become possible, at several levels. The first step is trying to get rational emergency reference levels for food. However, if one country drinks four times as much milk per head as another, one really does not expect the permissible level for milk to be the same in both countries; but the politicians insist that it should be. Another difficulty will be that the early decisions were all made very cautiously, and large changes may be required.

The International Atomic Energy Agency, the International Commission on Radiological Protection and the World Health Organisation are all considering longer-term discussions which, to be done properly, ought to take several years.

Questioner

Could you enlarge on the long term environmental effects of Chernobyl?

Dunster

The problem with the long term situation is that if the soil gets contaminated, the radioactivity grows through the roots back into the crops in subsequent years. This is not so significant as direct deposition on the growing crops, because there is a dilution factor at work. But there is a continuing exposure to people over a period of probably tens of years.

What the Russians have done inside the 30 kilometre region is not yet clear. They have certainly done some bulldozing of soil, and some deep ploughing to try and stop the dust blowing around. But personally I do not believe they are seriously considering growing crops inside the 30 kilometre radius for a long time. At longer ranges they have taken decisions basically to wait and see. They have banned milk and foodstuffs at various radioactive concentrations in the foods. For 1986 this poses a significant problem for them in terms of food production. I think they are taking the line that for subsequent years it is something which they will have to live with.

The modelling of how much goes back through the environment is very dependent on the type of environment. The Russians have some areas with a combination of woodland and pasture land where caesium, which is the main problem, moves through the environment in a more mobile way than is common in pasture land—and they expect that to give them problems. They talk about modifying their agricultural techniques by ploughing in absorbants that will retain the caesium, but this seems unlikely to contribute a big factor.

Wright

The picture one has been given is that a substantial fraction of the release was in the form of nuclear fuel that went high into the atmosphere, and came straight down again. So the most contaminated area was within the nuclear power station site itself, which is where they have concentrated their decontamination.

Dunster

That decontamination has proved fairly easy just because it was particles of fuel. If one can collect the particles one can do the decontamination. It is not like trying to clean something off a surface to which it has become intimately connected. Some of their successful decontamination appears to be the result of sweeping up the particles of fuel.

Walker (RTZ, London)

Can reassurance be given that an accident like that at Chernobyl couldn't have happened in the West, even if a number of operators had acted in the way that the Russian operators did?

Wright

It certainly could not happen with our operating reactors in the UK. We are talking about events where the positive void coefficient played a very important role, so physically something akin to Chernobyl could not have happened here. But more deeply, and more importantly, it just *would* not happen here. We are talking not about operator errors, but about operator malpractices. The culture is so different that I can assure you that people would never have behaved like that on a CEGB station.

The whole background is that our operators are far from being casual about the thing that they are controlling. They would not take those risks. We would know if risks like that were ever being taken. I can assure you that they are not, because I have inspectors who go and observe stations. It is against the law to breach any operating rule.

Price

Could you please clarify one point: does Magnox catch fire in carbon dioxide if it melts?

Wright

Yes it can do, but graphite does not.

Walker

The positive void coefficient is a very strong argument; but can we be told that, even if our people behave like idiots, we have done our homework so well that there is no hazard?

Price

Are the reactors 'operator-proof'—just as everything in the Navy has to be 'sailor-proof'?

Tanguy

In Electricité de France we are reaching conclusions needing a somewhat different presentation. We accept the idea that there will be operator errors and regulatory violations—not deliberately of course. So we cannot guarantee that there will not be a severe accident in one of our plants. We have done our best to prevent it; we consider that it is very unlikely; but we cannot give a 100% guarantee that an accident would not occur. But, now that we know what happened at Chernobyl, we can *guarantee* that it will never be a Chernobyl type accident, in terms of radioactive release. And we are quite sure that the design we have provided guarantees that the release would be of the order of less than 1% of what was released at Chernobyl. That would still be a serious accident, but much less serious for the population. This understanding works well around the nuclear plants already in commission. People understand that nuclear power is not risk-free, but that there are direct benefits; and they trust the EdF operator to handle and manage correctly an accident if it happened. This understanding does not work quite so well at the national level.

Dunster

I do not believe that view would be acceptable to our Nuclear Installations Inspectorate in the UK. An absolute guarantee of containing down to 1% of the Chernobyl accident is something I do not believe can be given. The mechanism for achieving a large release is not easy to postulate; but it is equally difficult to exclude totally. I do not believe it can be done. The risks are very low; the probability is very low. The possibility of a major release was considered in the Sizewell inquiry; it was taken into account; probabilities were put on it; but those probabilities were not zero.

Tanguy

This has been the subject of intense discussion for the past three years. It means that you have to exclude some given physical events, which are possible in theory, but where all experts agree that they will not take place in practice. The best example is in the case of core meltdown. If we do not exclude the possibility of an event so energetic that there could be an explosion ruining the huge containment building within (let's say) 1 hour, this would give rise to a release of Chernobyl magnitude. (By the way, I hope that everybody realises that with the Chernobyl accident, we have probably witnessed what could be the worst accident for a nuclear power plant.) This was ruled out in France due to our specific containment building design, with a very large volume and concrete and steel lining. If the French equivalent of the nuclear inspectorate would not accept that, we would not be able to present a case to the public. But in France the regulatory authorities have accepted this technical conclusion. It was the same thing for the hydrogen explosion. It is important that people stop looking for new physical phenomena. Physicists have done a good job. We know all of them and take them into account.

If you always tell the public about low probabilities then they will get the feeling that you are hiding the truth behind the use of probabilistic analysis. They want to know—yes or no—if it is 100% excluded to have a Chernobyl-level release.

Messer (RWE, Essen)
On a different subject: I believe the Russians have a chance to make a very important contribution to knowledge, to measure and determine the negative impact on health of small doses over a long period of time. Do you feel that the results would be sufficiently reliable?

Dunster
As far as the evacuated population of 135 000 is concerned, they do contain enough high dose groups and enough low dose groups to make comparisons possible. It is fairly likely that these groups will show differences in long term behaviour of the thyroid. I think there will be some observable non-fatal cancers and some non-malignant thyroid nodules. It is likely that there will be an excess of leukaemia in the high dose groups (for high dose I mean something in the region of $0.3-1.0$ gray; these are comparable with the bottom end of the Horishima–Nagasaki doses). I think over the next few decades positive numbers will come out of that group. For total cancers, I rather doubt it. I think the excess of total cancers is not likely to be enough to be observable, because something over 10% of that 135 000 will die of cancer anyway, and one would be only looking at most for a few thousand on top of that, more likely a few hundred. So there is really no likelihood of getting much information on cancer in general; but we should get something about thyroid, and something about leukaemia. Out-

side those areas it will all be theory: there will be no observable effects, nor would one expect them. There will not be negative findings; there will just be non-significant findings.

Whether the Russians can do this depends very much on their medical attitude. At the moment they have 135 000 patients, and they are very anxious not to treat them as statistics. The more carefully they look at them, the more thoroughly they examine them, and the more supportive medical treatment they get, the more likely they are to find something in that group. There may be false positives as a result of what one of the Russians called 'hyperdiagnosis'. That is a very real risk, and it has to be offset by looking at the low dose groups, who we trust are being treated as thoroughly. Whether the Russians have the right expertise I am not sure; I think they probably do. Considerable pressure was put on them to make this an international exercise, and they seemed to welcome the idea. They welcomed the idea, in particular, of some sort of international workshop to look at how that type of study should be conducted.

Questioner

I should like to ask about possible accidents in Third World countries.

Tanguy

This is an old question. It is a real problem, but we should keep in mind that Three Mile Island did not happen in Taiwan or Korea or in countries which are sometimes quoted as not having a long-established technological culture: it happened in the USA. Chernobyl happened in the USSR. If the question had been asked before Chernobyl, we would certainly not have included the USSR as a country with a less than satisfactory technological culture. Spain is an interesting case. I know that Spain is not a developing country. But when France sold a reactor to Spain in 1966, at that time there were also questions as to whether this type of reactor (a Magnox type) might present operating problems to them. Since that time, we in France have had two serious incidents in our plant, while Spain was able to avoid both of them. Having said that, I fully agree that it is a serious problem. We discussed it with other electricity producers, for instance in the Institute of Nuclear Power Operations, and have concluded that we have the responsibility at least to offer auditing services to electrical utilities which are operating only a limited number of plants, and which may not have sufficient expertise within their company. By this I mean a very detailed visit by people well aware of operational problems, scrutinising the way in which the plant is operated, and offering recommendations. If the exercise is to be useful these recommendations must have some kind of mandatory character. Some utilities have already approached INPO. China has approached EdF to get this type of assistance. It implies of course that they recognise that they do not have in-house the complete means to discharge their safety responsibility. I think a solution has to be found in this way, because the main responsibility will always rest on the operator.

Wright
I agree with what has been said, The main lesson is that we need a good infrastructure. If people are operating nuclear power stations without an adequate degree of expertise behind them, that is a very dangerous thing. I personally take comfort from the fact that some of the airlines in developing countries have a very good safety record, even though there are others where one perhaps would not be so happy to fly.

Units and conversion factors

Radioactive intensity
Radioactive intensity (in bequerels) is the number of nuclei disintegrating per second.

The old units were curies: 1 bequerel = 2.7×10^{-11} curie.

Absorbed dose
Absorbed dose (in grays) is the energy absorbed per unit mass of target matter (in joules per kilogram).

The old units were rads: 1 gray = 100 rad.

Dose equivalent (or dose)
Dose equivalent (in sieverts) is the absorbed dose (in joules per kilogram) multiplied by a factor for the particular type of radiation, which takes into account its effectiveness in causing damage.

The old units were rem: 1 sievert = 100 rem.

Prefixes
milli	thousandth	kilo	thousand
micro	millionth	mega	million